Advance Prais

MW00861577

"If your organizational leaders seek to engage Jewish Millennials — and who doesn't? — I highly recommend you make this important book by Rabbi Dan Horwitz a must-read together with your professional and lay leadership team. Here, you will learn the key concepts that powered the incredible success of The Well, the "B-branded" engagement initiative of Temple Israel in Detroit, Michigan. Beginning with the core principle that "relationships are everything," you will learn how coffee dates are vital points of connection, how co-creation leads to innovative gatherings like "#Friendseder," how to launch Shared Interest Groups, how to pay for it all by avoiding the word "free," and much, much more. The "takeaways" from each chapter provide a road map for creating your own path to building the Jewish future. Terrific and inspiring!"

Dr. Ron Wolfson, Fingerhut Professor of Education,
American Jewish University; Author, *Relational Judaism*

"Chock full of important insights and innovative tools for engaging Millennials in Jewish life, this book is a must-read for Jewish professionals and for anyone who cares about the future of the American Jewish community."

Sarah Hurwitz, Author, *Here All Along*

"JUST JEWISH is a worthy addition to the new Jewish bookshelf that is catalyzing new thinking and practices for the Jewish future we're just beginning to build. Much is unfamiliar in the new Jewish landscape but with imaginative practitioners like Rabbi Dan Horwitz our collective future can still be vibrant and compelling."

Rabbi Rick Jacobs, President, Union for Reform Judaism

"Rabbi Dan Horwitz, through his work with The Well, shined a bright light on the largely unfulfilled promise of engagement with Jewish Millennials. This book, which should be required reading for all who are engaged in Jewish community building, will help light the way for the rest of us."

Doron Krakow, CEO, JCC Association of North America

"To anyone who has sought to understand the black box of engaging Millennials, JUST JEWISH is a must-read! Thank you Rabbi Dan for sharing your playbook of success with all of us. This book will shape the conversation as to how we think about the Jewish future."

Rabbi Elliot Cosgrove, Park Avenue Synagogue, NY;
Editor, *Jewish Theology in Our Time: A New Generation
Explores the Foundations and Future of Jewish Belief*

"When I visited The Well, I was envious. Why wasn't my post-college life like that? And The Well felt enticingly hip and innovative compared with any bricks-and-mortar pulpit. Now some of The Well's Torah is available for all of us. Don't 'program for;' build with. Don't hawk 'membership;' weave relationship. Build a 'B-Brand,' nourish pluralism, and don't fear change. I emerged from this book ready to roll up my sleeves and build my own rabbinate better than before.
Rabbi Rachel Barenblat, aka "The Velveteen Rabbi"
Author, *Texts to the Holy*

"Rabbi Dan Horwitz claims to be writing about Millennials and the Jewish future. In essence his book is about a growing number, if not a majority of American Jews in the present. In authoring this book, Dan has also masterfully applied his unique perspectives to identify the current trends and patterns of normative Jewish behaviors that can be aptly applied to many Jewish communities and a wide variety of Jewish institutions. Importantly, Dan is not scared of penning what many may be thinking, but seldom have articulated in such a public forum. Having known Dan and his work for over a decade, his growth as a leader and changemaker has also been evident, learning from many, but mostly from the people he has served with such passion, respect and integrity."
Dr. David Bryfman, CEO, The Jewish Education Project

"There are few Jewish leaders who have devoted more thought to and spent more personal time on the critical issue of engaging Millennial American Jews than Rabbi Dan Horwitz. In an engaging but fearless manner, Horwitz raises the tough questions about our communal challenges in engaging young leaders and provides thoughtful and nuanced suggestions for a path forward. JUST JEWISH should be considered required reading for anyone serious about the existential question of how to assure that American Jews remain connected to their identities."
Daniel Elbaum, North American head, The Jewish Agency for Israel

"I devoured JUST JEWISH in a single sitting—but I underlined, scribbled comments, and made notes in the margins because I knew I'd return to this book often, using it as a resource for years to come. Daniel Horwitz's real-life, real-time, on-the-ground experiences coupled with his wisdom, humor, and contemporary references create the ideal road map for how to ensure today's young adult seekers become tomorrow's grown-up torch-bearers for Jewish life. Daniel's book is a must-read for anyone who cares about the Jewish future."
Zack Bodner, CEO, Oshman Family JCC Palo Alto
Author, *Why Do Jewish?*

"There are hundreds of well-resourced synagogues and Jewish organizations that are trying to figure out how to attract Jewish Millennials to their programs and services. Rabbi Dan is one of a handful of teachers/spiritual leaders who has been a Pied Piper to Jewish Millennials. His book is filled with dozens of examples of how he has done that successfully. Anyone who cares about making Judaism attractive and compelling to Next-Gen Jews needs to read this book."

Rabbi Sid Schwarz, Director, Clergy Leadership Incubator (CLI)
Author, *Jewish Megatrends: Charting the Course of the American Jewish Future*.

"In JUST JEWISH, Rabbi Dan Horwitz provides a superb roadmap and guide to the Millennials, a generation of Jews that has generally remained distant from the traditional institutions and practices of Jewish life. Drawing from his incomparably successful experience, Horwitz wisely provides the necessary language and tactics for effectively engaging this unique generation. This is an essential book for those of us who care about the future of Jewish life."

Rabbi Peter Rubenstein, Emeritus Director, Bronfman Center
for Jewish Life at 92Y; Rabbi Emeritus, Central Synagogue

"As the ground shifts beneath the feet of Jewish institutions, this book provides a road map for how to navigate these seismic changes in our community and in our world. Rabbi Horwitz demonstrates a deep knowledge and understanding of what makes Millennials tick, and how to meet them where they are. He brings the reader into conversation with the most current research available while being honest about the challenges inherent in this work. This is an essential handbook for any religious communal professional from any faith background."

Rabba Rachel Kohl Finegold, Moriah Congregation, Deerfield, IL

"Rabbi Horwitz has given today's Jewish communal leadership an invaluable roadmap to a strong and vibrant future. Meticulously researched and cogently argued, this book should be on the desk of every rabbi, cantor, Jewish professional and lay leader committed to the survival and renewal of American Judaism."

Rabbi Yonatan Dahlen, Congregation Shaarey Zedek, Southfield, MI

"JUST JEWISH is well-researched, highly accessible, and packed with valuable insights, compelling readers to consider their assumptions and open up important conversations about how to navigate the changing Jewish landscape. For leaders who want to build communities of belonging that help young people feel excited and proud to be Jewish, this book is required reading!"

Kohenet Keshira HaLev Fife, founder of Kesher Pittsburgh and
former Executive Director of Kohenet Hebrew Priestess Institute

"As a rabbi who ran a very large Jewish young adult project in Boston and now as the founder of Modern JewISH Couples, I am grateful for Dan's book which lays out the strategies, practices and pedagogies critical to working with the Millennial population. Not only was Dan a great colleague in this work, but The Well demonstrated creative models for young adult engagement that inspired my work and that of many others. But these models are not just for Millennials; they are adaptable to other populations that you might serve. The Jewish future depends on thoughtful leaders building models of rich Jewish learning, joy and relationships. Dan shares deep insights in innovation, engagement, and Jewish wisdom that are a beautiful blueprint for building vibrant Jewish community in the years to come. From Tot Shabbat to Friendseder, from meetings over cups of coffee to hosting Jewish learning gatherings in 3rd spaces, from fundraising from foundations to building participant investment, this book will help you in your work to make Jewish communities of meaning inclusive of Millennials and beyond."

Rabbi Jen Gubitz, Founder, Modern JewISH Couples

"From the moment I met him (some ten years ago) I knew that Dan Horwitz was the kind of transformational leader so desperately needed by our contemporary faith community. That sense has only been reinforced over and again in our work together. And now he has written this book which will serve as an authoritative guide to anyone concerned about the next generation and their commitment to the Jewish future. That should be all of us."

Rabbi Terry Bookman, EITZAH
Author, *Beyond Survival*

Just Jewish
How to Engage Millennials and Build a Vibrant Jewish Future

Rabbi Dan Horwitz

Ben Yehuda Press
Teaneck, New Jersey

Published by Ben Yehuda Press
122 Ayers Court #1B
Teaneck, NJ 07666
BenYehudaPress.com

To subscribe to our monthly book club and support independent Jewish publishing, visit Patreon.com/BenYehudaPress

Ben Yehuda Press books may be purchased at a discount by synagogues, book clubs, and other institutions buying in bulk.
For information, please email markets@BenYehudaPress.com

ISBN13 978-1-953829-49-8 paper; 978-1-953829-64-1 hardcover

23 24 25 / 10 9 8 7 6 5a   20240102

Dedication

For my parents,
the ultimate Jewish role models.

Contents

Foreword
by Rabbi Paul Yedwab

When I came to Detroit as a young rabbi in 1986, I purchased my first professional suit at Hudson's, the anchor department store in our local malls at the time. Before long, Hudson's had disappeared from the retail map... or so it seemed. As it turns out, their parent company had inserted a "disruptor" into the retail environment. It was an experiment to see if they could capture a new younger clientele with lower priced merchandise. They did not actually go out of business; rather, in the year 2000, they simply changed their name to that of their more successful disruptor. Today, they are known as Target!

In 2014, the largest Reform congregation in North America, Temple Israel of Metropolitan Detroit, made the decision to insert a disruptor into the local Jewish spiritual environment. With the help of a generous donor, Lori Talsky, and a determined and talented founding director, Rabbi Dan Horwitz, The Well was born. While The Well has not yet supplanted Temple Israel, it may very well provide us with a way forward in our efforts to engage this Millennial generation of fiercely independent, membership-resistant, digitally fluent Jews.

Since The Well is independently branded, people often ask me what Temple Israel gets out of the arrangement. The answer is: absolutely nothing, unless you count markedly raising the level of Jewish involvement for thousands of young Jews in our area in the belief that a "rising tide raises all ships." If we can fill those years between college graduation and nursery or religious school registration for their children with meaningful Jewish experiences, Temple Israel will be the beneficiary along with all the other congregations and Jewish institutions in our area.

We will also be the beneficiaries of the innovations that come from this much nimbler and less constrained outreach organization. Just one example: Since The Well does not charge "dues," Dan was in a quandary about how to financially support his ambitious staffing goals for the organization, especially since it was important to the founding donor that The Well's participants have "skin in the game." To fix this, Dan crafted an online fundraiser which thanked each donor on The Well's social media platforms with personally directed and moving posts. Why didn't we think to do that? Well, now we have.

Based on the excellent engagement models of synagogues like Temple Israel of Boston and their Riverway Project, we knew that we could have created a young adult organization more closely tied to our synagogue, but we wanted The Well to be a truly communal entity with no boundaries or labels. We wanted The Well's rabbi, staff, and lay leaders to have the ability to have "coffee dates" with anyone and everyone in the community. We wanted the Chabad-like freedom and mandate to engage Jews wherever they may be on their journeys. We wanted other congregations to buy in—and they have (some of them hesitantly at first), with many in the community now enthusiastically partnering with The Well on programs and religious services.

In order to create that sense of partnership with congregations, The Well had only three constraints. From the outset, we determined that the organization would not offer Hebrew School, Bar/Bat/B-Mitzvah, or High Holy Day services. The Well was not meant to supplant congregational life, but rather to eventually lead into congregational affiliation. With all due respect to Target, we really did not want to become Hudson's!

From many hundreds of individual coffee dates to a large-scale, community-wide, *Tashlich* program celebrated annually, to an inspired Jewish text study model to #Friendseder and holiday themed escape room experiences, not to mention weaving together dozens of small groups, The Well has become an innovation engine for our community and indeed the nation.

As the grandfather of The Well, I was honored when Dan asked me to write the foreword to this book about Millennial engagement. But rather than a foreword, think of this as an invitation. If you are a congregational rabbi, a Federation, JCC or other Jewish agency executive, or a lay leader in the community, it is time to dig more Wells in our Jewish communal landscape. For our Well has proven to be a deep and nourishing one.

Because of Dan's unique set of leadership skills, some have opined that The Well's success was dependent on his leadership. Great leaders, however, are those who can create organizations that can thrive without them. Such has been the case with The Well, which has been expanding its mission and reach under the able stewardship of Rabbi Jeff Stombaugh. So, you can do it; it is replicable. More importantly, it is vital, and the core takeaways in this book are a great way to embark on that Well-digging process!

In biblical times, the well was the communal gathering place. In Metro Detroit, it has become very much the same: a central address for collaboration, outreach, and innovation. So, dig a Well in your own community; you will not be sorry. Our brick-and-mortar-based models are weakening. Plant a disruptor in your own community—dig your own Well—and hit your "Target" of vibrant and expansive Jewish life for decades to come.

Introduction

Liberal Judaism's Tefillin Cart

Bind them as a sign on your hand and let them
serve as a symbol on your forehead.
—Deuteronomy 6:8

In 2009 I had the privilege of staffing a Birthright Israel trip.[1] After a handful of glorious days full of hummus and devoid of sleep, our bus of roughly 40 Millennials arrived at the *Kotel*—the Western Wall.[2] For those who don't know, the *Kotel* complex is divided like an Orthodox synagogue, with separate sections for men and women to congregate and pray.[3] As I escorted the male Birthright participants to the men's section, we were met by a Chabad[4] emissary standing alongside a *tefillin* cart.[5] The question the emissary asked when approaching each member of our group was: "Is your mother Jewish?" Those who answered *yes* were invited to wrap *tefillin*. Those who answered *no* were not invited to wrap *tefillin*, as they were not

---

[1] Birthright Israel is an organization that for over two decades has provided free 10-day trips to Israel for young Jewish adults.

[2] The Western Wall of the ancient Temple Mount is deemed by many the holiest site in Judaism.

[3] While there has been a movement to establish an egalitarian section for prayer in the Kotel plaza, as part of a broad coalition of actors seeking a "Kotel compromise," current Israeli political realities have not allowed for the plan to be implemented. In the meantime, egalitarian prayer takes place in an area outside the formal plaza known as Robinson's Arch.

[4] Chabad is a Jewish ultra-Orthodox Hassidic sect that has, as a driving principle, embraced outreach to non-Orthodox Jews around the world to encourage and inspire them to adopt an Orthodox lifestyle. The name itself is an acronym, drawn from the Jewish mystical tradition known as Kabbalah, and stands for "Wisdom, Understanding, and Knowledge."

[5] There isn't a great English translation for *tefillin*, but they're also known as phylacteries. Essentially, two little boxes containing Torah verses handwritten on parchment, one placed on your forehead and the other on your bicep, with leather straps coming out of them that are wrapped around you as you offer morning prayers on weekdays. Traveling with them through TSA checkpoints is an adventure! For more on Chabad's global *tefillin* campaign, see: Sue Fishkoff, *The Rebbe's Army* (Schocken Books, 2003), 46.

considered Jewish according to traditional interpretations of Jewish law.[6] I saw the devastated look in the eyes of a number of young men on the trip whose fathers were Jewish but whose mothers were not, realizing for the first time that their Jewish status was perceived as lesser-than by some Jews. This interaction took place right before a moment they had been so looking forward to. Instead of excited, they approached the *Kotel* feeling rejected, all but eliminating the opportunity for a deep Jewish spiritual experience.

In that moment, I wanted to scream: "Where is liberal Judaism's *tefillin* cart?!" Obviously due to the monopoly over the site by the *Rabbanut*—the Israeli Orthodox Rabbinate—space would never be created for a competing cart. But I couldn't help but wonder and wish that the more liberal streams of Judaism would bring greater intention to reaching out and connecting with Jews wherever they may be on their journeys—with an expansive definition of who constitutes a Jew, and an embrace of the non-Jews who they love and who love them.

The memory of that experience stayed with me, and a few years later, I put together a concept paper that laid out a vision of what a distinctly liberal Jewish outreach organization might look like. How could we take the best practices from the Jewish world, including techniques used by Synagogues, Federations, JCCs, Chabad, Hillel on Campus, Moishe House and more, and build an organization targeted to the needs of Millennials (who largely were not associating or affiliating with our community's institutions), while embracing a radically inclusive posture?

As with all things, timing is everything, and in the aftermath of the Great Recession,[7] it wasn't right. But a few years later, thanks to a se-

---

[6] Traditional Jewish law deems only those who are born of a Jewish mother (or who have formally converted) to have Jewish status. This is commonly referred to as being of matrilineal descent.

[7] "Two Recessions, Two Recoveries." Pew Research Center, Dec. 13, 2019, www.pewresearch. org/social-trends/2019/12/13/two-recessions-two-recoveries-2.

rious investment by a visionary donor, Lori Talsky, mentorship from one of the country's leading rabbis, Paul Yedwab, and the backing of the largest Reform Temple in the world, Temple Israel, the stars aligned such that we were able to bring the concept paper to life.

The Need

Over the years, there are a handful of questions that have been regularly posed to me by those who lead Jewish organizations and by the parents and grandparents of Millennials:

> "Why aren't Millennials donating to or serving on the boards of Jewish organizations the way their parents and grandparents did?"
> "Why aren't Millennials joining synagogues?"
> "Why aren't my Millennial children doing Jewish the way I did Jewish?"
> "Are there any books that focus on Jewish Millennial engagement and education post-college, sharing strategies and best practices from the field?"

For a religion that is hyper-focused on *l'dor v'dor*—transmitting the Jewish tradition "from generation to generation"—the notion that Millennials aren't interested in carrying on Jewish practices or embracing the Jewish commitments of those who came before them poses quite a challenge, both on interpersonal and organizational sustainability levels. As a result, it seems much of the Jewish organizational world is concerned with how to engage Millennials in their offerings. But, if the data collected from reliable sources such as The Pew Research Center are any indication, there is much more work to do.

Enter The Well, founded in the summer of 2015 in Metro Detroit to embrace this specific call to action, which has been doing on-the-ground research and development for Jewish Millennial engagement and education ever since. Repeatedly recognized as one of the 50 most innovative Jewish organizations in North America and included in the Slingshot Fund's inaugural "10 to Watch" list in 2020, with funding from both local and national donors, several models created by The Well have been embraced by organizations nationally. From custom Jewish holiday-themed escape rooms that have been licensed out to other communities around the country, to a blitz fundraising model that has since worked for campus Hillels and JCCs, to a remixed approach to Jewish text study that was a semifinalist for the inaugural Lippman Kanfer Prize in Applied Jewish Wisdom and which received national philanthropic support to pilot in additional cities, The Well—never with an annual budget of more than $500,000 or more than four full-time staff—has helped to transform the Millennial engagement and education landscape in Metro Detroit and beyond.

This book will share proven techniques and models ready to be adopted by the Jewish world's myriad organizations, touching on branding, fundraising, programmatic approaches, relationship development, and more, extrapolating lessons from The Well to be applied to the Jewish community writ large. As older generations start to step back from Jewish communal leadership, the time to meaningfully engage Millennials to ensure future leadership pipelines and Jewish vibrancy is NOW, and this book exists to help make it happen!

Why Millennials Specifically?

Upon learning I was writing this book, several friends asked why I was writing about Millennials exclusively rather than also including information on Gen Z (those born 1997-2012), who in the years ahead will make up a growing portion of the "young adult" population (which I define as those ages 22-39). There are three core reasons this book focuses exclusively on Millennials:

First, there are only a few years worth of Gen Z-ers who currently fit into the "young adult" demographic, and because older Gen Z-ers have much in common with young Millennials, strategies designed for Millennials will generally work for older Gen Z-ers too.

Second, my comparative expertise is Millennials, and it felt disingenuous to write about a group I'm not as familiar with and haven't actively engaged on the ground to the same extent.

Third, Gen Z-ers are still quite young, many years away from assuming mainstream Jewish organizational leadership roles, while Millennials are ready to be engaged and to take on leadership roles now!

As Gen Z comes of age and makes up the majority of the young adult demographic in the years ahead, I'll look forward to reading all about their particular and unique needs from those who have worked to engage them on the ground.[8] But this book is focused on Millennials!

What To Expect in This Book

Each chapter is going to explore different topics relevant to Millennial engagement. They'll draw on my expertise as a Millennial who has staffed Birthright Israel trips, worked as a Jewish summer camp counselor, lived and studied with Chabad at the University of Michigan, worked for Michigan State University Hillel and Moishe House, founded and built The Well, has been the CEO of a large JCC, and has served as a rabbi of a large congregation. Chapters will begin with balcony-level observations and academic theory and

---

[8] The Jewish Education Project in New York has already commissioned initial research about Jewish Gen Z-ers, published in a March 2019 report called "GenZ Now." www.jewishedproject.org/genznow

will then dive into examples of how theory was put into practice at The Well. Each chapter will conclude with Core Takeaways, so you can synthesize the information shared, and Discussion Questions, so you can use each chapter as a jump-off point for conversations.

Chapter 1 provides a brief primer on Millennials, helping to frame everything that follows.

Chapter 2 focuses on the power of what Dr. Ron Wolfson has coined "Relational Judaism," and explores one-on-one coffee dating and Shabbat Dinners as key Millennial relationship-building tools.

Chapter 3 focuses on combating Millennial loneliness, and examines the power of small groups as well as immersive experiences.

Chapter 4 focuses on the strategy of building a B-brand for a Millennial generation that shuns labels,[9] and on the value of getting outside of our organizational buildings.

Chapter 5 focuses on shifting from a culture of offering programs to co-creating gatherings, both with Millennials and partner organizations.

Chapter 6 focuses on marketing and pricing tactics that attract Millennials, the need to educate toward philanthropy, and explores alternative financial models for our various organizations, with an emphasis on eliminating the term "Free!"

Chapter 7 focuses on fundraising techniques most likely to resonate with Millennials.

---

[9] The title of this book, *Just Jewish*, is drawn from the fastest-growing category of Jewish self-identification—one which rejects denominational labels.

Chapter 8 focuses on how to inspire Millennials to engage in traditional "Jewish learning" such as text study.

Chapter 9 focuses on contemporary Millennial theology, prayer, interfaith (but really interfaithless) couples, and Israel.

I want to emphasize that The Well is one of many organizations in the national Jewish startup ecosystem that has brought attention and intention to engaging Millennials. Our approach from the very beginning was to try to take what we perceived as the best parts of Jewish life across organizations and denominations and package them together in an inclusive way that would resonate with Millennials in Metro Detroit while allowing for ripples to be felt beyond. Over the years our methods were tweaked constantly, absorbing learnings from others doing the work in the field across the country, both from books and articles that were published contemporaneously and from like-minded partners. Our successes would not exist but for the many who came before us, and the many who have been thought partners, programmatic partners, and supporters. There are wonderful folks all over this country doing incredible work in this space!

I'm proud of the impact The Well has had, and that the organization, now under new leadership, continues to touch and enhance so many lives. Since departing The Well I've had the opportunity to test out many of the Core Takeaways of this book both as the CEO of the Alper JCC in Miami, as well as in my role as a rabbi at a large 900+ family synagogue, proving their replicability and capacity to positively impact our community's Legacy Organizations. In distilling the core lessons learned over the years when putting academic theory into practice on the ground and by sharing them widely, I hope to be as helpful as possible to those who are already doing, or want to start doing, this critical work. I hope that this book helps you think in new ways, triggers meaningful conversations, and contributes to the continued flourishing of the Jewish people.

chapter 1

A Quick Primer on Millennials

Just as my ancestors planted for me, I too
am planting for my descendants.
~ Babylonian Talmud, Tractate Taanit, Folio 23a

Like me, the overwhelming majority of "young adults" today are Millennials. Born between 1981 and 1996,[10] Millennials have overtaken Baby Boomers (born 1946-1964) as the largest living American generation[11] and are the largest generation represented in America's labor force.[12] There has been much research conducted over the years on Millennials and how they interact with Judaism and engage with Jewish community. A lot of that research is woven throughout this book, so you'll be introduced to it along the way, but here are some key points to keep in mind as we dive in:

Millennials generally aren't "joiners," hate labels, and aren't as involved in Jewish organizational life as previous generations were at the same age.[13] Fewer than a third of Millennials think attending

---

[10] Michael Dimock, "Defining Generations: Where Millennials end and Generation Z begins." Pew Research Center, Jan. 17, 2019. www.pewresearch.org/fact-tank/2019/01/17/where-millennials-end-and-generation-z-begins.

[11] Richard Fry, "Millennials overtake Baby Boomers as America's largest generation." Pew Research Center, Apr. 28, 2020. www.pewresearch.org/fact-tank/2020/04/28/millennials-overtake-baby-boomers-as-americas-largest-generation.

[12] Richard Fry, "Millennials are the largest generation in the U.S. labor force." Pew Research Center, Apr. 11, 2018. www.pewresearch.org/fact-tank/2018/04/11/millennials-largest-generation-us-labor-force.

[13] Steven M. Cohen and Ari Y. Kelman, *The Continuity of Discontinuity*. The Andrea and Charles Bronfman Philanthropies, 2007. www.jumpstartlabs.org/wp-content/uploads/2021/05/The-Continuity-of-Discontinuity.pdf, 18.

synagogue is important to being Jewish.[14] Millennials are looking for new ways to be involved,[15] and "would rather express their faith by talking to their friends than by attending synagogue."[16] Most Millennials are Digital Natives, meaning they have comfort and complete fluency with emerging technologies.[17] Half of Jewish Millennials are the offspring of interfaith marriages.[18] Millennials are more racially and ethnically diverse than older Jews,[19] and a significant number identify as Jews of Color.[20]

There is a tension for Millennials between the particular and the universal. Courtesy of modern technologies, such as the internet and air travel, the world is flat. As author and *New York Times* columnist Thomas Friedman explains: "Several technological and political forces have converged, and that has produced a global, Web-enabled playing field that allows for multiple forms of collaboration without regard to geography or distance—or soon, even language."[21] Jewish Millennials are globally connected, have mostly non-Jewish friends, and are living in interfaith households at an incredibly high

---

[14] Anna Greenberg, *Grande Soy Vanilla Latte with Cinnamon, No Foam...* Reboot, 2006. www.acbp.net/pdf/pdfs-research-and-publications/Latte%20Report%202006.pdf, 20.

[15] Ari Y. Kelman and Eliana Schonberg, *Legwork, Framework, Artwork.* Rose Community Foundation, 2008. https://rcfdenver.org/study-report/legwork-framework-artwork-engaging-next-generation-jews-june-2008/4.

[16] Jacob B. Ukeles. et al., *Young Jewish Adults in the United States Today.* American Jewish Committee, 2006. www.jewishdatabank.org/content/upload/bjdb/631/Young_Jewish_Adults_in_the_US_Today.pdf, 26.

[17] Digital Native is a term coined originally by Marc Prensky. "Digital Natives, Digital Immigrants Part 1." *On the Horizon,* 2001. Vol. 9 No. 5, 1-6. www.marcprensky.com/writing/Prensky%20-%20Digital%20Natives,%20Digital%20Immigrants%20-%20Part1.pdf.

[18] Theodore Sasson et al., *Millennial Children of Intermarriage.* Brandeis University, 2015. https://www.brandeis.edu/cmjs/noteworthy/intermarriage.html.

[19] *Jewish Americans in 2020* Pew Research Center, May 11, 2021. www.pewresearch.org/religion/wp-content/uploads/sites/7/2021/05/PF_05.11.21_Jewish.Americans.pdf, 175.

[20] For more on the unique experiences of Jews of Color, and in particular the discrimination they have experienced in the organized Jewish community, see: Tobin Belzer et al., *Beyond the Count.* Jews of Color Initiative, 2021. www.jewsofcolorinitiative.org/wp-content/uploads/2021/08/BEYONDTHECOUNT.FINAL_.8.12.21.pdf.

[21] Daniel H. Pink, "Why the World is Flat." *Wired,* May 1, 2005, www.wired.com/2005/05/friedman-2/.

clip (whether as the products of an interfaith marriage and/or in one themselves). As a result, it should come as no surprise that they tend to favor universal constructs.

But the world is a big place, comprised of over 8 billion people as of this writing.[22] To try and be in common cause and relationship with the entire world is an overwhelming concept. There thus remains an important role for particularistic community to play, and Millennials are willing to embrace the particular—so long as it's not to the exclusion of the universal.[23] Fortunately, as Rabbi Lord Jonathan Sacks (of blessed memory) taught, "Judaism is built on a dual structure. It has a universal dimension and particularistic one, neither of which negates the other."[24] The framing we need to provide for Millennials is that the particular (that is, being actively part of the Jewish community) can help them lead a healthier, self-actualized, and meaningful life. The particular is where we go to recharge our batteries—to feel supported, uplifted and inspired—in order to then go out and effect universal change, working toward justice and equity for all the inhabitants of the world.

Millennials are not monolithic and fall into 3 distinct life stages: 1) Single, 2) Coupled, and 3) Parents.

1. **Single**: These folks are actively seeking their life partners or are simply enjoying being single. Marriage is not a given for Millennials, and when it does happen, it tends to happen much later than in previous generations.[25] This has certain

---

[22] United Nations, Population, www.un.org/en/global-issues/population.

[23] Shlomi Ravid, *Engaging Millennials with Jewish Peoplehood*. Center for Jewish Peoplehood Education, 2016. www.jpeoplehood.org/wp-content/uploads/2016/06/Peoplehood17-updated.pdf, 13.

[24] Jonathan Sacks, *Future Tense* (Schocken, 2012), 212.

[25] Amanda Barroso et al., *As Millennials Near 40, They're Approaching Family Life Differently Than Previous Generations*. Pew Research Center, May 27, 2020. www.pewresearch.org/social-trends/2020/05/27/as-millennials-near-40-theyre-approaching-family-life-differently-than-previous-generations/.

upsides, such as lower divorce rates,[26] and certain down-sides, such as a greater likelihood of fertility challenges.[27] Those who are seeking a partner often avoid singles events. Millennials generally prefer to be introduced via mutual friends, to meet someone in a social setting comprised of folks of varying relationship statuses, or to "match" via smartphone dating applications.[28]

2. **Coupled:** These folks are in serious committed relation-ships, are engaged, or are married. The needs and desires of couples are different than singles. For example, dinner clubs are a much more attractive way to spend your time once you've found your romantic partner. And who doesn't love a leisurely brunch date? It's important to note that not every couple is interested in having children and suggesting that procreation is the expectation is offensive to some. It's also important to be sensitive to the fact that many couples may be trying to have children but are struggling to do so.

3. **Parents:** Parents are in an entirely different life stage, with much of life now focused on keeping little humans alive and cared for. Their time is at a premium! As Rabbi Nicole Auerbach notes, "Parents of school-age kids are the hard-est people to engage; they feel like they don't have another extra minute in their day."[29] Many Millennial parents are happy to participate in Jewish life if the experiences are designed to include their children and are affordable. But

---

[26] Ben Steverman, "Millennials Are Causing the U.S. Divorce Rate to Plummet." *Bloomberg*, Sep. 25, 2018. www.bloomberg.com/news/articles/2018-09-25/millennials-are-causing-the-u-s-divorce-rate-to-plummet.

[27] "About 1 in 5 (22%) couples in which the woman is 30-39 have problems conceiving their first child, compared to about 1 in 8 (13%) couples in which the woman is younger than 30. Fertility declines with age primarily because egg quality declines over time." Centers for Disease Control and Prevention, Infertility FAQs. www.cdc.gov/reproductivehealth/infertility/index.htm.

[28] Bella Gandhi, "7 dating tips to steal from millennials." *TODAY*, June 7, 2017. www.today.com/health/how-millennials-date-today-t112431.

[29] Ron Wolfson and Brett Kopin, *Creating Sacred Communities* (The Kripke Institute, 2022), 88.

for parents to participate in Jewish communal gatherings designed exclusively for adults, those gatherings must be exciting enough to be "babysitter-worthy," as just leaving the house has the associated cost of needing to hire a babysitter. And to have them give of their limited time to help co-create a gathering (that is, to attend planning meetings and feel ownership over it), they need to be really excited about it! It's important to remember that not all parents are coupled, whether due to divorce, choosing to have a child on one's own, or other reasons.

There is often as large as a 20-year gap between a young Jewish person finishing college[30] and the time they might consider enrolling their eldest child in a Jewish nursery school (which for many is their next Jewish organizational touchpoint). There historically has been a continuous arc of sorts as it relates to how Jewish life might unfold for those connected to the organized Jewish community: Jewish nursery school, followed by day school or supplemental "religious school" or "Hebrew school" and a Bar/Bat/B-Mitzvah,[31] teen youth group, and then Hillel on campus when one goes to college.

For the Baby Boomer generation, it wasn't uncommon for folks to get married and begin growing their families soon after finishing college, meaning the gap between college graduation and enrolling their kids in a Jewish nursery school—thus starting the cycle over—was shorter. But with Millennials on average getting married later (if at all), having children later (if at all), and then having to make the decision to educate their children Jewishly (of which there's no

---

[30] The overwhelming majority of young Jewish people attend college: "Jewish Educational Attainment." Pew Research Center, Dec. 13, 2016. www.pewresearch.org/religion/2016/12/13/jewish-educational-attainment.
[31] Bar Mitzvah ("son of the commandments") and Bat Mitzvah ("daughter of the commandments") are gendered terms. B-Mitzvah serves as a gender-neutral alternative for the growing number of teens with gender identities beyond the binary.

guarantee after a 20+ year gap in Jewish involvement), there are potentially decades' worth of Jewish growth, communal participation and leadership being missed out on, to the detriment of both Millennials themselves and our community more broadly. While many of our community's organizations strive to have an "open door" to Millennials, the reality is these doors are often "an open door no one can find."[32] Even when the open doors can be found, many of the services offered within simply aren't what Millennials feel they need in their lives.

The primary organization that has emerged to fill this post-college, pre-nursery school enrollment gap is Moishe House. Founded in 2006, Moishe House is now the global leader in engaging young Jewish adults in their 20s and is a mainstay in Jewish communities around the world. The core Moishe House model is to subsidize the rent of groups of 3-5 young Jewish adults to live in a house together, to provide them with a modest programming budget and staff support, and to empower them to host around half a dozen events each month open to the young adults in their city, be they Shabbat dinners, holiday celebrations, movie nights, bar nights, sporting events, Jewish text studies, community service projects—whatever! The vision is to empower young Jewish adults in their 20s to build the Jewish communities they want to be a part of. The organization has scaled tremendously over the years and has been a game-changing addition to the Jewish organizational landscape. Moishe House is where I cut my own professional teeth and began my direct work with Millennials, as at the beginning of my rabbinic career I served as their organizational rabbi and had the privilege of building out their Jewish education and immersive experiences platform.

While working for Moishe House, I couldn't help but wonder if there were similar but distinct models that could have just as significant an impact. For example, Moishe House events are tradi-

---

[32] Terry Bookman, *Beyond Survival* (Rowman & Littlefield, 2019), 125.

tionally planned and executed by laity—that is, the people living in the houses. What would it look like to have a professional working with them in a co-creative relationship to enhance the substantive content included in their programs and provide additional resources? Moishe House residents often move out of their house after a couple of years (often due to Millennial transience, burnout from hosting so regularly, or having found a romantic partner they now want to live with), and many who attend events at their local Moishe House do so because they're friends with one of the people who lives in the house. This means that for many, only a couple of years out of the targeted two decades are being filled with Moishe House experiences. Research has shown that those experiences have a significant and lasting impact,[33] but what could the other 15+ years during this crucial time look like for those folks? And where might a relationship with a rabbi fit into the picture?[34]

Having wrestled with these questions, we launched The Well in Metro Detroit to serve as a bridge between the life stages. Using a distinctly inclusive lens, we hoped to inspire Jewish Millennials to feel connected with the Jewish community so when the time came there would be no question that they would want to educate their children in a Jewish setting and/or live Jewishly active lives, and to then facilitate handoffs to our community's Legacy Organizations. Tactically, we decided we would do this by building personal relationships (in particular, with a rabbi), by actively weaving together micro-communities within our larger community, and by using a co-creation model that empowered our community's Millennials to

[33] Moishe House: 2018 Evaluation Findings. Informing Change, 2018. https://issuu.com/rachel23elizabeth/docs/moishe_house_executive_summary_5.16. Moishe House has recently brought the Base Movement under its umbrella, which puts couples—at least one of whom is a rabbi—out into the field to do outreach and community building work. A different model than their core model, and both are running beautifully simultaneously! Check out https://basemovement.org.

[34] We learned from our independent evaluation commissioned in Year 5 that having a connection with the rabbi was a key factor for many participants.

create and facilitate the gatherings they wanted to partake in, cultivating the community they wanted to be part of.

A moment ago, I used the term "Legacy Organization." What do I mean by that? In the Jewish philanthropic world, it's common to think of nonprofit organizations as fitting into one of three distinct lifecycle stages: 1) Start-Up, 2) Mezzanine, and 3) Legacy. Start-Up Organizations generally are just getting off the ground and are building out their organization and its services. Mezzanine Organizations tend to have established a track record of success and are focused on capacity building to ensure they can continue delivering those services in the long run and/or to expand their reach courtesy of their successes. And Legacy Organizations are those that have established brands, clientele, sophisticated governance, and more.[35] Generally, I think of Start-Up Organizations as under 5 years old, Mezzanine Organizations as those between the ages of 5-15, and Legacy Organizations as those that have worked toward fulfilling their missions for over 15 years. Throughout this book, when I use the term "Legacy Organizations," I'm generally referring to organizations that are well established in the Jewish community, have been around for more than 15 years, and are "mature" as it relates to the organizational lifecycle, such as most synagogues, JCCs, Federations, and the like.

It may not be a popular opinion, but I don't think that Legacy Organizations should continue to exist just because they already exist. Models that were well suited to address the needs of 20th-century Jews need not necessarily be the models that speak to those coming of age in the 21st century. Jewish communities have migrated over the years, and in some of our communities we remain wed to physical buildings that are no longer central or convenient to where Jews are living. Consolidation, mergers, and even closures of Legacy

---

[35] "Life Cycle Stages." Slingshot, 2019. https://slingshotfund.org/life-cycle-stages/.

Organizations are not signs of weakness, but signs of change in the marketplace, requiring careful thought about how our community's finite resources are allocated. There is a vibrant Jewish innovation sector which has resulted in hundreds of creative Start-Up organizations seeking to meet the needs of contemporary Jews. Rather than being frustrated or scared by newcomers to the scene, my hope is that our Legacy Organizations will pay close attention, take note of the successes, and "borrow" their best practices or even bring the fledging disruptors under their own organizational umbrellas as financial parents or as acquisitions, providing needed funding and access to resources to help them grow and succeed.[36]

There were several folks over the years who were confused as to why we'd structure The Well to focus on the needs of Millennials specifically. Terms like "ageist" were certainly used, generally by folks in their 40s, 50s and 60s who wanted to participate in our offerings but were politely rebuffed. Those same folks would recognize that attending a local high school youth group event, or a women's health and fitness club like Curves if they were a man, would be inappropriate. Different subsections of people have different needs, and generational distinctions are real.[37] It's okay to curate spaces meant for some and not others. Not every organization needs to serve every person—even when your organization bills itself as "inclusive." We were establishing an organization with a mission, and that mission was focused on the unique needs of Millennials. As a result, we benefited from what Rabbi Elie Kaunfer refers to in his book *Empowered Judaism* as "youthful energy, youthful appeal."[38] And we were keen on protecting that appeal, because as any parent

---

[36] For a great example of this, check out the Marlene Meyerson JCC acquiring Immerse NYC: www.forward.com/life/409055/the-mikveh-is-the-trendy-place-to-be-in-manhattans-upper-west-side

[37] If interested in learning more about generational distinctions, and in particular how they play out in the workplace, I highly recommend the book *When Generations Collide* by Lynne C. Lancaster and David Stillman.

[38] Elie Kanfer, *Empowered Judaism* (Jewish Lights, 2012), 18.

can tell you, the surest way to make something uncool for young people is to have their parents embrace it. Just ask Facebook![39]

That said, I want to emphasize that there is power and value in intergenerational communities, which have been a primary Jewish communal organizing principle for many years. After all, the transmission of Judaism *l'dor v'dor*—from generation to generation—can only happen when different generations are spending time together so cultural transmission can take place! So while I think it's valuable to have spaces where subgroups can congregate independent of one another, I also think it's important for relationships and conversations to take place across the generations.

One of the things that makes synagogues so special is that you can have several generations in attendance, celebrating, learning, teaching, and singing together. Studies have shown there are significant benefits to being part of such communities. For example, in a time where teen mental health is a mainstream topic, research has shown that "youth who feel that many adults care about them tend to have the highest levels of development and the fewest interpersonal relationship challenges."[40] Teens in an intergenerational community have that many more adults who know and care about them. My congregation's senior citizens melt at the sight of little ones running up to the *bimah*[41] to get a lollipop from the rabbi at the end of Shabbat morning services. Fostering opportunities for multiple generations to be together is incredibly important, so The Well hosted at least a couple of intergenerational gatherings each year. But our core focus was Millennials—a generation you hopefully know much more about now!

---

[39] Helen Lewis, "What Happened When Facebook Became Boomerbook." *The Atlantic*, Oct. 5, 2021. www.theatlantic.com/ideas/archive/2021/10/facebook-midlife-crisis-boomerbook/620307.

[40] Michael Ben-Avie et al., *"Learning and Development of NFTY Teens."* North American Federation of Temple Youth, 2007. https://www.bjpa.org/bjpa/search-results?search=Learning+and+development+of+nfty+teens, 4.

[41] The elevated platform from which prayer services are traditionally conducted.

Core Takeaways

1. Millennials fall into 3 distinct life stages, are more than likely the products of an interfaith relationship or are in one themselves, and are more racially diverse than previous generations.
2. Millennials will embrace the particular, provided it isn't to the exclusion of the universal.
3. To attract parents of young children, gatherings must be babysitter-worthy.
4. For many Millennials, there are often as many as 20 years between college graduation and reconnecting with Jewish life as an adult.
5. There's a need for generational subgroups to gather. There's also a need for intergenerational community.

Discussion Questions

- Does our organization differentiate in our outreach to Millennials depending on their life stage? If so, how? If not, why not?
- How is our organization planning to attract and welcome a comparatively diverse generation?
- How do we make sure the gatherings we plan are "babysitter-worthy"?
- What subgroups do we currently cater to, if any? When does it make sense for them to have their own space and time? How and when do we work to bring everyone together?

chapter 2

Your Teeth Are Stained

He (Moses) burned it in fire, ground it to
powder, strewed it upon the water,
and made the Israelites drink it.
—Exodus 32:20

"Rabbi Dan, I don't know how to tell you this, but your teeth are stained. Like, unbelievably stained. It took the hygienist twice as long to polish them as it would a normal person. How much coffee are you drinking?"

These words, offered to me by my dentist at my annual cleaning, made me smile. A huge, stained-teeth smile. Little did he know that in the year leading up to that visit, I had been on over 300 one-on-one coffee dates with Jewish Millennials in Metro Detroit. Now, the truth is that I have never had a cup of coffee, except for one time as an undergraduate studying abroad in Jerusalem when I accidentally brewed an Israeli instant packet of "Nescafe" that I thought was hot chocolate. For some reason, coffee never clicked with me. It smells amazing, I'll give you that. But the flavor is bitter and doesn't match the smell, which I've always found odd. In any case, when it comes to how I prefer to consume my caffeine, I'm a tea drinker. When I shared that fun fact with my dentist, he laughed, and shared with me that tea stains teeth even worse than coffee! I thought back to an art project in elementary school where we used tea leaves to stain white parchment paper to make it look older, and it all began to make sense. For each of my annual cleanings thereafter we scheduled extra time with the hygienist, as coffee dating was a core pillar of our work at The Well.

Cultivating relationships one-on-one is the first core step in meaningfully connecting with Millennials (and frankly, with anyone). As my teacher Dr. Ron Wolfson writes:

> It's not about programs. It's not about marketing. It's not about branding, labels, logos, clever titles, website or smartphone apps. It's not even about institutions. It's about relationships.[42]

Relationships are everything. A recent Harvard University study concluded that personal connections are the most important factor in long-term health and happiness.[43] The best way to start building a personal relationship with someone is by spending quality time with them. According to social psychologist Harry T. Reis, the central organizing principle of cultivating enduring relationships is "perceived partner responsiveness." That is, "our relationships are stronger when we perceive that our partners are responsive to us."[44] And as Rabbi Lydia Medwin teaches, "there's actually not a more efficient way to help people feel seen and heard and known than having a one-on-one conversation with them."[45] There is tremendous power in being with another person, making them feel like they're the most important person in the world to you at that moment, and using the connection to begin building a relationship of trust. What better way to do that than over a cup of coffee (or tea)?

---

[42] Ron Wolfson, *Relational Judaism* (Jewish Lights, 2013), 3.
[43] Robert Waldinger and Marc Shulz, "The Lifelong Power of Close Relationships." *The Wall Street Journal*, Jan. 13, 2023. www.wsj.com/articles/the-lifelong-power-of-close-relationships-11673625450.
[44] Chip Heath and Dan Heath, *The Power of Moments* (Simon and Schuster, 2017), 231.
[45] Ron Wolfson and Brett Kopin, *Creating Sacred Communities* (The Kripke Institute, 2022), 82.

We took coffee dating so seriously that written on the back of my business card was: "Redeem this card for a coffee with Rabbi Dan!" and The Well's alternate logo featured the Spirit of Detroit statue[46] wearing one of our t-shirts, holding a menorah in one hand and a coffee cup in the other. Marisa Meyerson, The Well's Director of Operations, shares that "[t]aking the time to hold these one-on-one conversations and develop relationships with the people in our community is absolutely vital to the success of The Well—I'd say it's part of our secret sauce. For us, these coffee dates are simply a part of our daily work routines; I couldn't imagine working for The Well without doing them."[47] Coffee dating was a team effort—something everyone was expected to do as part of their jobs. We even provided a budget for our board members to go on coffee dates, empowering them to represent us in the community, and having them play a significant role in our outreach efforts.

Over the course of more than 5 years, I went on well over 1,500 coffee dates. Add in the hundreds and hundreds more each year facilitated by my teammates and board members, and we easily topped 2,500 coffee dates over 5 years. We even considered investing in a coffee shop at one point, as it may have been more economical and might have provided a meaningful revenue stream for the organization!

Why Coffee Dates are Amazing

So, what is it about one-on-one coffee dates that make them such an impactful engagement tool?

First, they're low pressure. The meeting takes place in public, alleviating any fears the person you're meeting might have about being

---

[46] For more on the Spirit of Detroit, visit: https://historicdetroit.org/buildings/spirit-of-detroit.

[47] Marisa Meyerson, "The Coffee Philosophy: Building an Intentionally-Welcoming Community." Slingshot, Apr. 28, 2020. https://slingshotfund.org/post/the-coffee-philosophy-building-an-intentionally-welcoming-community.

alone with someone they don't know—because they're not alone! Even if there are no other customers in the shop, the barista is there. And if the meeting ever feels uncomfortable, they can simply stand up and leave.

Second, coffee shops are well-suited for relaxed conversations. The music isn't particularly loud and the people aren't particularly rowdy, especially when compared to a bar. There are many Jewish organizations that use the lure of "free alcohol" to try to attract people to their events. From the beginnings of The Well, we intentionally embraced coffee shops—both for one-on-one coffee dates and as venues we'd rent out to host larger gatherings.[48] We did this for two reasons: we didn't want to make assumptions about peoples' relationships with alcohol (that is, we wanted to be sensitive to anyone who might be struggling with addiction); and because alcohol consumption often clouds judgement, we wanted to protect our representatives and those they were engaging from any inappropriate (or perceived as inappropriate) boundary crossings. For many years, The Well didn't rent office space, so coffee shops served as our offices too!

Third, for most people, the topic they most enjoy talking about is themselves! This is especially true when they feel someone is actively listening to them. So, when peppered with questions about their lives, interests, Jewish journeys and more, most Millennials are more than happy to share about themselves with you. The adage that "God gave you two ears and one mouth for a reason" is incredibly important advice when coffee dating. Listening more than speaking creates space for the person across the table from you to speak at length about themselves and feel a sense of connection with you. Our organizational coffee dates were scheduled to last 45 minutes. If

---

[48] I prefer the term "gatherings" to "programs" and will regularly use it throughout this book. To my ear, a program is transactional, while a gathering is something you're a part of. As we shift from transactional to relational constructs, our language choices should ideally follow suit.

they weren't going well for some reason, we could cut them short to a half hour. If they were flowing, we could extend them to an hour. The goal was to never have the time together feel rushed; we wanted to make it clear that we didn't have anywhere more important to be in that moment than with that person, learning as much about them as we possibly could and beginning to build a personal relationship. After a quality coffee date, personal outreach and invitations became possible, and the potential participant now had an anchor person at gatherings, even if they didn't have other friends to attend with just yet.

Coffee Dating Challenges

While coffee dates are an incredible relationship-building and engagement tool, they come with their own set of potential challenges. For example, some people don't want to meet with a rabbi. They look suspiciously at "religious" people, believing their goal is to trick them into becoming more religious themselves. There were coffee dates where it was clear the person across the table was suspicious of my motivations. At least one person asked me outright: "Why do you want to take me, a person you don't know, out for a coffee, if not to try to make me change something about myself or do something I'm not currently doing?" There were also some coffee dates that clearly resulted from parents or grandparents insisting that the person meet with me. Jewish guilt is a thing! It's hard to begin to build a relationship if the person you're sitting across from isn't excited about sitting across from you, and it's one of the many reasons that I wasn't the exclusive coffee dater as our team grew. Don't want to meet with the rabbi? No problem! Between our staff and board, we had someone who was a solid coffee-dating match for just about anyone, allowing us to be strategic matchmakers. When we had a disengaged Jewish Millennial we were hoping to weave into community, we selected a coffee-dater to represent us based on age, life stage, personality, energy level, intensity of Jewish background/ observance, and more. We wanted people to have their first touch point with The Well be with someone they were going to click with that they would be excited to befriend.

As discussed in Chapter 1, Millennials are not monolithic. There is a significant gap within the generation when it comes to technology. The oldest Millennials remember a world before cellphones and the internet. For instance, my first cellphone was gigantic and lived in my teal 1994 Plymouth Voyager hand-me-down minivan's glovebox. It used a pre-paid $50 calling card, and my parents made clear that it was to be used for emergencies only. On the other hand, most Millennials are Digital Natives—they are far more fluent with the internet and technology, having been raised from a young age surrounded by it. They often seek to connect digitally before connecting in person. In fact, a large majority of Millennials communicate more digitally via text messaging applications than they do in person on any given day.[49] As a result, sitting down and having a conversation with someone in person, with eye contact and without a device in hand, is countercultural for many and exercises a skill set that they often haven't practiced and that feels unnatural to them. As Tiffany Shlain writes in her book 24/6: "Eye contact is the first and last form of communication we have. It's fundamental. And I worry we're losing it."[50]

It was evident that some of the Millennials we coffee-dated were more comfortable engaging in an in-person conversation in polite fashion than others. There were several conversations where it admittedly felt like pulling teeth given the lack of conversational skills. One-word answers, no eye contact, text messaging others during our

---

[49] Rurik Bradbury, "The digital lives of Millennials and Gen Z." *LivePerson*, 2017. http://liveperson.docsend.com/view/tm8j45m.
[50] Tiffany Shlain, 24/6 (Gallery Books, 2020), 93.

conversation, and other similarly not ideal behaviors presented from time to time. There were also folks with social anxieties and general shyness, folks who were neuro-divergent, and folks with different cognitive abilities, all of whom we warmly embraced and worked hard to build relationships with.

Another challenge to coffee dating is that many Millennials still work the traditional "banking hours" of 9am-5pm. So, in order to be able to meet Millennials for a one-on-one coffee, we needed to accommodate their schedules, requiring night and weekend hours. One of the greatest challenges of Jewish professional life is that in addition to putting in standard daytime hours, many Jewish engagement professionals are putting in additional time on nights and weekends. While there are some organizations that try to address this by allowing their staff to work fewer daytime hours, by providing comp time, and/or providing a day off during the middle of the week, my impression is that most Jewish engagement professionals are working traditional hours and also nights and weekends, which leads to burnout. Coupled with concerns about inadequate pay and staffing,[51] it's no wonder that a 2016 Leading Edge survey found that a majority of Jewish communal professionals were planning on leaving their current jobs within 5 years.[52]

The night and weekend hours can also cause problems when it comes to having a social and/or family life. It's important to draw boundaries. But if a potential participant was only able or willing to meet at 8:30pm on a particular Tuesday at a coffee shop a 30-minute drive away, we'd find a way to make it happen.

---

[51] "Are Jewish Organizations Great Places To Work?" *Leading Edge*, 2021. www.leading-edge.cdn. prismic.io/leading-edge/4abae90f-97b5-45a2-8bd1-96dca60b89bc_2021+Employee+Experien ce+Survey.pdf, 4.
[52] "Are Jewish Organizations Great Places To Work?" *Leading Edge*, 2021, 22.

Coffee dating best practices

(courtesy of The Well team members
Avery Markel and Marisa Meyerson)

- Arrive early. Scout out a place to sit. Welcome your coffee date warmly when they arrive, order your drinks together, and pay for both.
- Ask open-ended questions. Listen more than you speak. Find the balance between being interested and being interesting.
- Before the meeting, check out your coffee date's public-facing social media to see who your mutual friends are, where they went to school, etc. If they've been in the news or published articles, read (about) them and come prepared with questions or reflections.
- Leave your assumptions at the door.
- If the goal of the coffee date is to empower someone to take on a leadership role, have a few opportunities ready to share with them while they're excited.
- Follow up with them after!

What Comes Next?

So, you've gone on a coffee date with someone you're hoping to engage in your organization. What comes next?

The big mistake many make is to simply invite that person to their next organizational gathering without demonstrating that they internalized what the person shared with them on the coffee date. Targeted outreach is key! I cannot overstate how important it is to intentionally choose the first gathering you invite the person to join to be one that will align with their expressed interests. As Well participant (and now rabbinical student) Sarah Klein shares, "We are not just serving people, but human beings with passions, ideas, needs, and desires."[53] Tailoring invitations to the person you're reaching out to is essential!

When you reach out personally with an invitation, you can say, "I think you're really going to appreciate this upcoming gathering, and I would love for you to join me there. I remember during our coffee date that you expressed a passion for 'x,' which ties in beautifully with this gathering." The person will be much more likely to attend now that they (a) have received a personal invitation, (b) the gathering is targeted to an expressed passion of theirs, and (c) it came from someone they're forming a relationship with who has demonstrated they actively listened to them.

So, for example, if during the course of your coffee date a person says that they are turned off by prayer services, don't have your first outreach to them after the date be to invite them to a Shabbat prayer experience—even if that's what's next on your organizational calendar, or you think that the way you do prayer is such that it might change their minds. Instead, reflect on what they expressed an interest in and strive to have the first organizational touchpoint post-coffee be one that aligns. If they love community service, invite them to a service project. If they love learning about new topics, invite them to an event featuring an expert guest speaker. You'll have a better chance of long-term success engagement-wise if their first touchpoint with your organization beyond the coffee date is one that speaks to their existing passions.

What should you do if you're not sure what the appropriate gathering is to invite someone to (or if you are sure, but it's many weeks or even months away)? The answer is surprisingly simple, and it embraces one of the most powerful (and delicious) vehicles for community and relationship building that we have in the Jewish world: invite them to Shabbat dinner.

---

[53] Sarah Klein, "Finding My Tribe at The Well." Slingshot, Apr. 14, 2020. www.slingshotfund.org/post/finding-my-tribe-at-the-well.

Shabbat Dinner

Shabbat is at the core of Judaism, and there is no shortage of commentary on its importance. For example, Zack Bodner writes in his book *Why Do Jewish* that, "We could consider Shabbat the single greatest religious invention of all time."[54] Author Sarah Hurwitz notes in *Here All Along* that, "[W]hen time isn't carved up into tiny slices for meetings and calls, or constantly interrupted by tweets and texts, it takes on a different texture."[55] And in her book *Remix Judaism*, Professor Roberta Rosenthal Kwall writes that, "Shabbat['s]... celebration on a weekly basis has tremendous potential to safeguard Jewish tradition in a world of increasing secularization. It allows for a much-needed break from our fast-paced existence by carving out sacred time and space on a consistent basis..."[56]

One of the key features of Shabbat for many is a leisurely Friday evening meal. Essentially, a weekly dinner party! While there are specific rituals traditionally associated with the evening, they are simple and brief, allowing for the evening to flow with uninterrupted conversation. Who wouldn't want the chance after a long work week to gather with quality people for good food, drink, and conversation? As a result, Shabbat Dinner is programmatically at the core of many of the organizations most respected for effectively engaging Millennials. Moishe House was born when a group of recent college graduates in the Bay Area hosted a Shabbat dinner for their friends.[57] Hillel on Campus and Chabad have used Shabbat dinners for decades as a primary engagement tool. And now, there's One-Table, an organization whose mission is to empower young adults "to find, share, and enjoy Shabbat Dinners, making the most of their Friday nights."[58] So, when thinking about how to effectively weave

---

[54] Zack Bodner, *Why Do Jewish?* (Gefen Publishing House, 2021), 170.
[55] Sarah Hurwitz, *Here All Along* (Random House, 2019), 160.
[56] Roberta Rosenthal Kwall, *Remix Judaism* (Rowman & Littlefield, 2022), 21.
[57] More on the founding of Moishe House here: www.moishehouse.org/about-us/our-story.
[58] www.onetable.org/about-onetable-shabbat.

Millennials into community, inviting them to Shabbat dinners is a no-brainer!

We experimented with several different approaches to hosting Shabbat dinners over the years, using both our home and rented venues, home-cooked vs. catered vs. potluck meals, and group sizes ranging from six to hundreds of people. The gatherings that were the most successful at weaving people into community were not the large-scale catered ones hosted in trendy venues. Contrary to what many think, large group settings often aren't the best place to meet new people. The most successful gatherings were the ones we hosted at our home, with a home-cooked meal, catering to a group of roughly 12 people who had been invited because we believed they would hit it off and form fast friendships with one another.

We found providing a home cooked meal was particularly valuable. Aside from compelling academic research indicating that the more home-cooked meals one eats the healthier one tends to be,[59] cooking for our guests had them feeling cared for, nourished, and imagining what they might cook if they were to host a Shabbat Dinner. Practically, this meant that my wife and I had to spend significantly more time preparing for the meal than we otherwise would have, but that investment of time, effort and dollars was recognized by our guests, and helped set the tone for our shared time together.

In addition to helping to foster friendships, hosting Shabbat Dinners allowed us to model how to make Shabbat special and a regular practice in one's life as we encouraged our guests to find personal meaning in the associated pre-meal rituals.[60] Courtesy of the ritual portions of the evening being simple and brief, Shabbat Dinners

---

[59] Susanna Mills et al., "Frequency of eating home cooked meals and potential benefits for diet and health: cross-sectional analysis of a population-based cohort study." *Int J Behav Nutr Phys Act.* 2017 Aug. 17; 14(1):109.www.ncbi.nlm.nih.gov/pmc/articles/PMC5561571.

[60] Shabbat Dinner pre-meal rituals traditionally include: lighting candles, blessing the wine, washing one's hands, and blessing the challah. Some also bless their children (if applicable) and sing a song of love and gratitude to their spouse (if applicable).

also provide a low barrier to welcome interfaith couples into Jewish spaces. As Ed Case, the founder of the Center for Radically Inclusive Judaism notes: "Interfaith families have consistently found marking Shabbat to be particularly meaningful."[61]

Hand Washing

Outside of the Orthodox world, the practice of ritually washing one's hands before breaking bread has largely fallen out of practice. This handwashing is traditionally done to mimic the priests in the ancient Temple in Jerusalem, who would wash their hands before offering up sacrifices. For many, this isn't a particularly compelling reason to embrace the ritual now. Yet there's beauty in inheriting a millennia-old ritual. Rather than simply discarding it, we aspired to inspire folks to find personal meaning in it.

For example, my personal take on ritual handwashing is twofold. First, the conclusion of the one-line blessing offered is *"al netilat yadayim"*—"on the raising of the hands." So, each week on Friday night after washing my hands, I think of my favorite techno song, Fedde Le Grand's "Put your hands up for Detroit," and raise my hands up in the air to celebrate my hometown. Second, there's a custom before washing to remove any hand jewelry you might be wearing, such as rings. So, each week, after washing our hands and putting our hands up for Detroit, my wife and I place one another's wedding rings back on each other's ring finger in a recommitment to one another and our partnership. In doing so, we infuse new personal meaning into an ancient ritual. What's stopping you from doing the same?

For some of the Millennials we invited to our home, a plated dinner party was not something they had experienced before. After all, at campus Hillels, Moishe Houses, and Chabad houses, you generally don't need to make an advance commitment of any kind

---

[61] Edmund Case, *Radical Inclusion* (Center for Radically Inclusive Judaism, 2019), 53.

to attend a Shabbat Dinner. If you feel like showing up, you show up! However, this is frustrating for those hosting such a dinner, who need to determine how much food to purchase and prepare, how many people to set tables for, etc. There were times when I reached out with a personal invitation to join us at our home for Shabbat Dinner a few days beforehand and was met with a "Oh cool, thanks, I'll try to make it." I then would have to let the person know that I needed a firm yes or no commitment, as there were limited seats at our table, and "I'll try to make it" wasn't an acceptable answer.

Admittedly this was hard for some. Getting Millennials to commit to something in advance can be challenging, with the generation being known for its lack of willingness to commit to things (jobs, romantic partners, and social plans included). This is due to what is commonly referred to as FOMO: Fear Of Missing Out.[62] FOMO works like this in the Millennial mind:

> "I could commit to doing this one thing, but what if something cooler or more interesting comes up after I've made that commitment? And what if all my friends are doing that other thing? And then I have to see pictures of them being happy on social media doing that cool thing that I missed out on? Instead of committing to something, I'd rather keep my options open."

This is the case even if it means they end up on the couch scrolling through their phone while watching Netflix because nothing more interesting came along. So much focus is placed on the "cool factor" that many organizations successfully catering to Millennials

---

[62] There's a great television episode of *Broad City* titled "Hashtag FOMO" (Season 2, Episode 5) that is worth watching to get a better sense of how FOMO often plays out for Millennials.

actively ask when designing experiences: "What is this event's Instagram-able moment?" That is, what about this gathering is going to inspire Millennials to take out their phones, take a picture or selfie, and share it to their social media so that they can show off having attended, and so that their friends who didn't attend will feel like they missed out and will want to attend the next event?

While we used that marketing tactic for The Well's larger, forward-facing gatherings that were open to all, we did not embrace an open-door policy or worry about Instagram-able moments for our intimate, invitation-only Shabbat dinners. Rather, we wanted to limit the size of the group and not go crazy trying to figure out how much food to prepare or how many places to set. This approach is championed by author Priya Parker, who shares in her book *The Art of Gathering* that 12 people is an ideal group size for dinner parties, as it's small enough to build trust and intimacy and large enough to offer a diversity of opinion.[63] She also emphasizes that having the right mix of people in the room is key to success and that sometimes, in order for a gathering to achieve its goals, we must kindly exclude others.[64] In other words, allowing people to attend at random may defeat the purpose of the gathering, even if it feels good or lends itself to the Jewish value of *hachnasat orchim* (welcoming guests)—or, as I often hear my Christian friends phrase it, the notion that "there's always room for another chair at the table."

It was challenging at times to turn folks away from our Shabbat Dinner table due to their unwillingness to commit to attending in advance. But as word got out about The Well, and as people heard from others about the experiences they were having and the people they were enjoying meeting, when invited to Shabbat Dinner at

---

[63] Priya Parker, *The Art of Gathering* (Penguin, 2018), 51.
[64] Parker, 35.

our home, most Millennials accepted and appreciated that we were curating groups with intention.

One of the most challenging things about hosting Shabbat dinners frequently is the toll it takes on those hosting. In the Chabad model, couples are in on the work together and are compensated accordingly. In our case, my wife had her own full-time job and was not an employee of The Well, yet she regularly partnered with me in cleaning, shopping, cooking, preparing the table, and hosting. Once our second child joined the family, it was clear that continuing to host as frequently as we were would burn us out. We also realized that we were missing out on an empowerment opportunity. While hosting in our home was great, we wanted to empower folks to host their own Shabbat Dinners so that they too could fall in love with hosting, in turn making Shabbat Dinner a regular part of their lives.

So, after joining us for a Shabbat Dinner in our home, attendees were invited to host in their own homes. We provided coaching, resources, potential guests, an accessible blessings sheet, and more; our staff team would even make a brief appearance to help facilitate rituals if that was something the hosts were stressed about. The result was that the number of Shabbat Dinners we supported as an organization tripled year over year, and several of our Shabbat Dinner Shared Interest Groups were born (more on this in Chapter 3)!

The 5 Steps

We've established that coffee dates and Shabbat Dinners are key steps for building relationships with Millennials, and that targeted rather than blanket event invitations are essential in order to have Millennials feel you've actively listened to them. These three steps formed the core of The Well's 5-step approach to moving folks from being uninvolved in Jewish communal life to being actively involved and taking on leadership roles:

1. **Coffee Date**.
2. **Shabbat Dinner invitation** with goal of facilitating new friendships.
3. **Targeted invitation** to an upcoming gathering.
4. **Weave the individual** into a Shared Interest Group meeting monthly.
5. **Empower the individual** to co-create a gathering.

These steps didn't always happen in this exact order, and not every step was appropriate for each person we engaged. People are unique, and our approach to each person needed to be as well. Some folks already active in the Jewish community came to us with ideas for gatherings they were hoping we'd help them execute, so they effectively jumped right in at Step 5. Others had no desire to make an ongoing monthly commitment, so Step 4 wasn't in the cards. Wherever people were on their journeys, we were prepared to meet them.

Rabbi Mike Uram, in his book *Next Generation Judaism*, defines two broad categories of Jewish Millennials: (1) Empowerment Jews, and (2) Engagement Jews. Broadly speaking, he defines Empowerment Jews as those who are already well-connected to Jewish spaces, while Engagement Jews are not connected to Jewish spaces and have a lower degree of Jewish association.[65] There are other intriguing frameworks that have been proposed as well (see, e.g., Rabbi Sid Schwarz's construct of Tribal Jews vs. Covenantal Jews[66]). Our work at The Well touched many Empowerment Jews, who we happily built relationships with and empowered to co-create with us. But

---

[65] Mike Uram, *Next Generation Judaism* (Jewish Lights, 2016), 19-20.
[66] Sidney Schwarz, *Jewish Megatrends* (Jewish Lights, 2013), 10.

our organizational tactics, including the 5 Steps mentioned above, were designed with Engagement Jews in mind.

It's important to note that our staff team made a point of going on "repeat" coffee dates with those we had already been on coffee dates with. We sought to deepen our personal relationships with the folks we were serving, even once they had been woven into community. It was often those subsequent one-on-one conversations that created the trust needed for us to weave them into a Shared Interest Group (Step 4), and/or to invite them to co-create an upcoming gathering with us (Step 5).

Humility

On some coffee dates, we recognized that the person we were sitting across from wasn't interested in what we at The Well had to offer, and that they would be more likely to connect with one of our community's other organizations. Whenever that happened, we facilitated introductions! Our team embraced being community concierges, helping people find their place in the Metro Detroit Jewish ecosystem. For example, we introduced those who were passionate about the environment and sustainability to our local Hazon representatives, and those who wanted to participate in ongoing community service projects to our local Repair the World team. We introduced those who wanted to be engaged in social justice work through a Jewish lens to the leadership of Detroit Jews for Justice. Not every organization needs to be the "home base" for every person—and frankly, no single organization can be. Our community is simply too diverse. Recognizing that other organizations may be better suited for an individual is not a weakness but a strength, and facilitating introductions in order to weave them into our communal tapestry makes our community that much richer!

Core Takeaways

1. Relationships are everything.
2. One-on-one coffee dates are an essential relationship-building tool. Just be sure to give your dentist a heads-up if you make them a habit!
3. Intimate Shabbat Dinners are a meaningful way to continue developing relationships. Bring intention to your guest list, invite guests you think will connect with one another, and be ready to not pull up an extra chair to the table.
4. When inviting someone to an upcoming gathering, choose one that will be of specific interest to them, and extend a personal invitation for them to join you.
5. Be ready and willing to facilitate introductions to partner organizations whose offerings may better suit someone's passions and/or needs.

Discussion Questions

- How does our organization go about building relationships of trust?
- What creative messaging might we place on the back of our business cards?
- In addition to our staff, which of our lay leaders can we empower to host intimate Shabbat Dinners with curated guest lists?
- How might we better track the passions of our people, so that we can bring intention to connecting them with others who share those passions?
- Do our staff and lay leaders have an understanding of the local Jewish community, and the organizations that comprise its ecosystem? Why or why not?

chapter 3

The 5 Best Friends Anyone Could Have

And God said, it is not good for the Human to be alone;
I will make a fitting counterpart for him.
—Genesis 2:18

The Torah begins with the Jewish people's narratives about creation. We learn how our ancestors perceived the world's birth and how they imagined God responding to the various creations. At the end of each act of creation, we find the refrain: "And God saw that it was good." Sun, moon and stars? God saw that it was good. Sea creatures? God saw that it was good. Land animals? God saw that it was good. Each step of creation presented in the Torah is deemed "good," until in Chapter 2 of Genesis we read: "And God said, it is not good for the Human to be alone; I will make a fitting counterpart for him." According to the Torah, human loneliness is the first "not good" thing in all of creation.

Despite being digitally hyper-connected across various social media platforms, Millennials are incredibly lonely. According to a 2019 YouGov poll (pre-pandemic), 30% of Millennials say they always or often feel lonely, and 22% say they have no friends.[67] Research is now clarifying what many had already assumed: that digital hyper-connection, and in particular the regular use of social media platforms where people are comparing their lives to the filtered lives

---

[67] Jamie Ballard, "Millennials are the loneliest generation." YouGov America, July 30, 2019. https://today.yougov.com/topics/society/articles-reports/2019/07/30/loneliness-friendship-new-friends-poll-survey.

of their "friends," is not just correlative but actually causes loneliness and depression.[68]

Millennials came of age as America's love affair with and commitment to civic and religious organizations crumbled, as documented by author Robert Putnam in his book, *Bowling Alone*. The rise of high-speed internet and streaming television has created more at-home entertainment options than ever before. In February of 2022, there were over 817,000 individual TV programs to choose from in the United States across the various streaming platforms, with the number continuing to grow.[69] Consumption of television courtesy of streaming platforms has become so embedded into Millennial life that a widely used euphemism for engaging in sexual activity with a partner is to invite them over to "Netflix and Chill."[70] The Covid-19 pandemic certainly did nothing to help combat Millennial loneliness and depression, with 92% of Millennials responding to a Blue Cross Blue Shield Generation Survey in 2020 saying that the pandemic had a negative impact on their mental health.[71] In a generation where people are often lonely or depressed, are spending much more time alone,[72] have more options than ever before to be entertained while sitting in sweatpants on their sofas, and with more companies now competing for their attention than ever before courtesy of our "attention economy,"[73] the likelihood that a Millennial is going to show up to a Jewish communal gathering by themselves is low.

---

[68] Melissa G. Hunt, et al., "No More FOMO: Limiting Social Media Decreases Loneliness and Depression." *Journal of Social and Clinical Psychology*, vol. 37, no. 10, Dec. 2018. www.guilfordjournals.com/doi/pdf/10.1521/jscp.2018.37.10.751.

[69] "State of Play." The Nielson Company, 2022. www.nielsen.com/insights/2022/state-of-play/.

[70] www.dictionary.com/e/slang/netflix-and-chill/.

[71] "Millennial Health: Trends in Behavioral Health Conditions." Blue Cross Blue Shield Association, Oct. 15, 2020. www.bcbs.com/the-health-of-america/reports/millennial-health-trends-behavioral-health-conditions#oldergen.

[72] Bryce Ward, "Americans are choosing to be alone. Here's why we should reverse that." *The Washington Post*, Nov. 23, 2022. www.washingtonpost.com/opinions/2022/11/23/americans-alone-thanksgiving-friends/.

[73] A concept developed by Nobel Laureate Herbert Alexander Simon, an American economist, political scientist and cognitive psychologist, which posits that since human attention spans are

I can't help but look back at previous generations and examine the kinds of social outlets they had courtesy of their civic and religious commitments. My late grandfather, a Traditionalist,[74] attended *minyan* (prayer services) at synagogue every morning. While I'm sure praying itself played some part in his rationale for attending, I'm confident that the modest breakfast immediately following the services that he shared with the other daily attendees played an even larger role. He got to spend time, in person, engaging in conversation with the same group of people every day. If he missed a day, someone would reach out to check in on him, making sure he was okay. If someone else missed a day, he would do the same for them. Courtesy of daily time spent together, the ability existed to get beyond the superficial subjects that often dominate "catch up" conversations, and to form deep bonds.

My parents, Baby Boomers, were weekly Saturday morning synagogue goers and brought my siblings and me along each week. While not equivalent to the ties my grandfather had with his daily group, we had a tight-knit community with whom we looked forward to sharing Saturday mornings. The kind of community in which you'd offer to drop off a meal when someone was sick, and where the kids were always spending time at each other's homes on Saturday afternoons, with an open-door policy.

I see most Millennials "doing Jewish" even less frequently, resulting in far weaker connections to the Jewish community. Some are finding community in other settings, but many are lacking meaningful communal ties beyond their families, losing out on the benefits, support and loneliness-combating magic that being part of a community brings.

---

limited, they are effectively a finite resource in the marketplace, and companies are in essence competing with one another for our limited attention.
[74] Also known as The Silent Generation, a term referencing those born between 1928-1945.

So, how do we inspire Millennials to participate actively in Jewish life? To get them excited about "doing Jewish"? The most effective way is to make sure they have Jewish friends, because it's having a friend to invite to join you, or who invites you to join them, that motivates people to leave their homes and go out into the world. Fewer than 30% of Jewish Millennials have all or mostly Jewish friends,[75] so even those who wouldn't identify as lonely and have lots of friends may not have friends to regularly "do Jewish" with. As Jewish educator Lisa Soble Siegmann observed to me, "It's like we're all still in 8th grade—we don't want to go to things without people we know!" Given these realities, The Well's big picture goal took shape: *We aim to introduce you to the 5 best friends you didn't know you didn't have (but secretly always wanted) to do Jewish and life with*. We were going to help Millennials make Jewish friends so that they'd always have someone to participate in Jewish activities with.

Five admittedly was an arbitrary number to choose, as we wanted people to have as many Jewish friends as possible. But five also felt like a stretch goal, so that we couldn't settle for helping folks make only one or two Jewish friends. More Jewish friends means a greater likelihood of being invited by them to do Jewish things, and a greater likelihood of having someone join you when you extend similar invitations to others.

Rabbi Irwin Kula teaches that religion is a toolbox for human flourishing.[76] That is, the purpose of any religion is to help people live the best lives they possibly can. Inspired by his framing, it was important to us that a person's new Jewish friends were people whom they could not only "do Jewish" with, but also "do life" with. Nothing made us happier than seeing people hanging out with people we'd introduced them to in secular social settings. Movies?

---

[75] "Jewish Americans in 2020." Pew Research Center, May 11, 2021. www.pewresearch.org/religion/wp-content/uploads/sites/7/2021/05/PF_05.11.21_Jewish.Americans.pdf, 111.
[76] Nicha Ratana and Saul Kaplan, "This Is Why Religion Is Just a Technology." *TIME*, July 25, 2014. www.time.com/3032104/religion-technology-irwin-kula.

Bowling? Picnic in the park? All amazing. It became a primary goal of ours whenever hosting a gathering to inspire those present to exchange cellphone numbers with one another, so that they could be in touch and spend time together afterwards.

In addition to helping Millennials find Jewish friends to "do Jewish" and "do life" with, it is important to create Jewish spaces where their non-Jewish friends and significant others feel welcomed and included! If a Jewish Millennial feels they can be their whole selves and include the people they love in what they're doing, they're much more likely to do Jewish. For non-Jewish significant others in particular, helping them find their people to do Jewish and life with—independent of their partner—allows them to establish their own connection with the Jewish community. Part of our communal strategy should be helping Millennials make more Jewish friends. The other part is making sure they know their non-Jewish friends and partners are welcome, encouraging the promising finding that "six-in-ten [US Jews] say they at least sometimes share Jewish culture and holidays with non-Jewish friends."[77]

Frequency and Flourishing

In 2020, the Pew Research Center released an updated version of its Portrait of the American Jewish Community. The gold standard in communal surveying, the final report contains hundreds of pages of charts and findings and is cited throughout this book. From the entire report, what most stood out to me was the finding that Jews with higher levels of traditional religious observance—defined as those who do at least 3 of these 4 things: host/attend a Passover Seder, fast for at least some of Yom Kippur, attend synagogue at least monthly, and/or keep kosher at home—are also much more likely than those with lower levels of traditional religious observance

---

[77] "Jewish Americans in 2020." Pew Research Center, May 11, 2021. www.pewresearch.org/religion/wp-content/uploads/sites/7/2021/05/PF_05.11.21_Jewish.Americans.pdf, 70.

to participate in Jewish cultural activities (such as listening to Jewish music, reading Jewish literature or newspapers, and watching TV with Jewish/Israeli themes).[78] I was also surprised to learn that those who responded they actively express their Jewishness in ways other than attending religious services are "consistently less engaged in Jewish life than are Jews who do attend religious services at least once or twice a month."[79]

While I'm aware of and appreciate the "cultural Jew" construct, I don't think I fully realized until reading the report that religious Jews are consumers of Jewish culture at a much higher clip than self-described cultural Jews are. Perhaps there's an argument to be made that Jewish cultural organizations striving to secure their futures should actively encourage Jews to take on a more traditional religious practice!

But what is it about these "traditional religious observance" markers that leads to greater participation in Jewish life? My take is that despite the framing of the four markers as religious, their observance and associated outcomes have little to do with theology or spirituality and everything to do with people doing Jewish on a regular basis. Traditional religious observance, as defined by the markers Pew identifies, means that one is doing Jewish at least monthly. If your 3 of 4 markers are monthly synagogue attendance, hosting or attending a Passover Seder, and fasting for at least part of Yom Kippur, then you're doing Jewish at least monthly (courtesy of monthly synagogue attendance). If you're keeping kosher at home, along with any 2 of the 3 other markers, you're doing Jewish daily, as at each meal you're making a Jewish choice. If you're regularly think-

---

[78] "Those who are low on the scale of traditional religious observance, meanwhile, tend to be much less active in the vibrant array of cultural activities available to U.S. Jews in the 21st century. In fact, no more than about one-in-ten low-observance Jews say they often do any of the dozen things mentioned in the survey." "Jewish Americans in 2020," 26.

[79] "Jewish Americans in 2020," 85.

ing about the fact that you're Jewish and are regularly doing Jewish, it stands to reason that you're more likely to engage in additional Jewish communal activities and be a consumer of Jewish culture.

The Pew data make it clear that frequency of participation in Jewish life matters and begets additional participation. Not all participation needs to be by attending large-scale gatherings—there is a need for more intimate experiences as well.[80] Occasional touches here and there are nice, but if we hope to have as many people as possible actively partaking in the incredible array of Jewish offerings that exist, in order to enhance their lives, provide a sufficient base of support for our communal creatives to express themselves, and allow real relationships to form, then we must strive to inspire at least monthly participation in Jewish life.

Shared Interest Groups

Knowing we aimed to introduce people to their 5 new best friends to do Jewish and life with, and knowing we wanted them participating in Jewish life at least monthly, The Well's Shared Interest Groups were born. The concept of weaving together groups of people to be in micro-communities is certainly not unique to The Well. There are many faith and secular communities that use small groups as a community-building technique. As Rabbi Lydia Medwin, a super-practitioner when it comes to weaving folks into small groups, teaches: "[S]mall groups are the most basic form of community."[81]

When designing The Well's Shared Interest Groups, we were inspired by the *havurah* model that began in the 1960s, and became mainstream in the 1970s:

---

[80] GatherDC's "Heartbeat Model" is a great way of framing this concept:Rachel Gildiner, "Relational Engagement During a Pandemic: GatherDC's Heartbeat Model." *eJewishPhilanthropy*, May 1, 2020. http://ejpprod.wpengine.com/relational-engagement-during-a-pandemic-gatherdcs-heartbeat-model.
[81] Ron Wolfson and Brett Kopin, *Creating Sacred Communities* (The Kripke Institute, 2022), 84.

"[H]avurot adopted 60s-era ideals—including egal-
itarianism, informality, cohesive community, active
participatory prayer, group discussion, and uncon-
ventional forms of governance. Participants met
weekly, biweekly, or monthly; sat in circles; dressed
casually; took turns leading worship and study; ate,
talked, and celebrated together; and participated in
the happy and sad moments of one another's lives—
one rabbi perceptively described the havurah as a
'surrogate for the eroded extended family.'"[82]

Over the course of a few years, using information gleaned from
many coffee dates, we wove together more than 40 Shared Interest
Groups, each comprised of 8-12 young adults or 4-5 young families meeting monthly. These included women's *Rosh Chodesh* new
moon circles, Shabbat Dinner groups, young family playgroups,
men's whiskey groups, charity poker giving circles, an Indian lunch
buffet exploration group, and more. Some were distinctly "Jewish" in
terms of their content, while others were not. But as Well lay leader
George Roberts writes:

The real Jewish-community building magic of our
Shared Interest Group comes after our monthly
whiskey meetings... The magic happens when one
member invites another member to attend a holiday
program that The Well is putting on, or when a few
of us get together for a Shabbat dinner, or when we
gather for a #Friendseder. Or... when it's a global
pandemic. And Passover. And you desperately need
Matzo.[83]

---

[82] Jonathan D. Sarna, *American Judaism* (Yale University Press, 2004), 321.
[83] George Roberts, "Running Out of Matzo in a Pandemic." Slingshot, Apr. 21, 2020. www.
slingshotfund.org/post/running-out-of-matzo-in-a-pandemic/.

Helping people find their people to do Jewish and life with ripples into robust Jewish community, even if the content of the monthly experience isn't distinctly Jewish.

Charity Poker Giving Circles

What's a "Charity Poker Giving Circle" you ask?

A "giving circle" is a philanthropic model in which a group of individuals contributes money to a pooled fund, learns together about various charities and each other's values, and makes collective donations to enhance impact. "Charity poker" is a fundraising vehicle for nonprofit organizations, which organize a poker tournament and skim a meaningful percentage of the entry fees off the top to support their bottom line.

The Well had piloted a giving circle in partnership with Amplifier Giving, the Jewish organization championing the model,[84] with participants finding great meaning in it. And one of the key indicators of social decline examined by Robert Putnam in *Bowling Alone* was the decreasing frequency of people gathering to play cards.[85] So, why not experiment with bringing the two concepts together?

We wove together groups of 12 young men who we believed would become fast friends. Each group member committed to hosting one of the year's monthly gatherings, where they'd be responsible for providing snacks and drinks. At each gathering, group members bought in for $20 and received $15 in poker chips, with $5 going to a side charity pot. The host took 5-10 minutes each evening to share about a charity particularly meaningful to them.

At the end of each one-year cycle, the group played a tournament-style game (which is distinct from the typical cash game in that there must be a single player who "wins" by being the last

---

[84] Amplifier has since been acquired by the Jewish Federations of North America, another great example of Legacy Organizations acquiring startups as discussed in Chapter 1. For more details about that acquisition: www.ejewishphilanthropy.com/the-jewish-federations-of-north-america-warmly-welcome-amplifier.

[85] Robert Putnam, *Bowling Alone* (Simon & Schuster, 2000), 104.

player standing), with the proceeds of the charity pot being donated to the charity the winner presented about when they hosted, and with the winner claiming the tax deduction. Learning about the charitable priorities of others is a meaningful way to get to know them on a deeper level and helps get beyond typical surface-level poker table banter about sports and politics!

Our approach, and the reason many of these groups are still gathering monthly more than 6 years later, is that we didn't randomly assign people into groups courtesy of their shared interests alone; we matched people up with those we felt they would form lasting friendships with. This admittedly is as much an art as it is a science, and there were times people we thought would hit it off did not, and groups we launched quickly came back down to earth. But in getting to know folks as individuals, courtesy of coffee dates, Shabbat dinners, gatherings, and more, we were able to get a good sense of each person's vibe—their way of being—and bring that to heart and mind when matching them up with potential new best friends.

The Well's Shared Interest Groups possessed a number of features that allowed for them to be amazing community-building vehicles:

First, we kept the groups small enough where intimacy was possible and large enough such that if a couple of people couldn't attend in a given month, the gathering would still be worthwhile.

Second, the groups were designed such that every group member was responsible for hosting at least once during the year, and when hosting was responsible for providing the food and drink. Since we didn't charge folks to participate in these groups, the agreement to host at least once a year was the "buy-in" that allowed for those in the group to feel a sense of reciprocity and mutuality of obligation. Participants having skin in the game is a must!

Third, these groups were lay-led; they gathered without requiring a staff person in attendance. Each group had a designated point-person who our staff would check in with after gatherings to solicit feedback, track attendance and the like. We made our staff team available to provide resources and coaching, and facilitated partnerships with organizations like OneTable, Moishe House Without Walls, PJ Library and At The Well (not to be confused with The Well!) to help provide the groups with additional financial and content resources. While there may have been some added value in a staff member facilitating the groups, empowering group participants to feel ownership and take turns as leaders allowed us to support a much larger ecosystem of groups than we would have been able to otherwise, reaching that many more people.[86]

Fourth, the groups met monthly. When inviting an ongoing commitment from Jewish Millennials, we found that a monthly commitment was palatable in a way that a more frequent commitment was not. Weekly or biweekly participation in a designated group simply wasn't attractive. However, courtesy of the monthly group commitment serving as an anchor, many then also participated in additional Jewish communal offerings each month!

Finally, these groups were all "closed." That is, the rosters were set, and new people were not permitted to join an existing group absent approval from all the group's members, which generally only occurred after an existing group member departed (remember: Millennial transience is a thing!).[87] While some were frustrated by what seemed an exclusionary policy (especially from an organization that describes itself as "inclusive"), this emotion stemmed from not understanding the purpose of the groups. Authors Chip and Dan Heath share in their book *The Power of Moments* that "to spark moments of connection for groups, we must create shared meaning."[88] It is through shared experiences—especially ones allowing for vul-

---

[86] For forward-facing (that is, open to anyone) gatherings, co-creation works best with Millennials! More on this in Chapter 4.

[87] Neale Godfrey, "The Young And The Restless: Millennials On The Move." *Forbes*, Oct. 2, 2016. www.forbes.com/sites/nealegodfrey/2016/10/02/the-young-and-the-restless-millennials-on-the-move.

[88] Chip Heath and Dan Heath, *The Power of Moments* (Simon and Schuster, 2017), 247.

nerability—that shared meaning is created. Randomly introducing new members to groups that had already been meeting for some time risked jeopardizing the shared meaning that had been established, and in turn a group's cohesiveness. To paraphrase author Priya Parker, we didn't want our Shared Interest Groups to end up hijacked in the name of politeness.[89] When we were approached by people who wanted to join a group that was already established, we shared with them that while the group was unfortunately closed, we would love to build a new group around them!

I mentioned Millennial transience a moment ago. I do think it's important to acknowledge that Metro Detroit is one of the more insular Jewish communities in the United States. According to the community's 2018 demographic study, 66% of Jewish adults in Metro Detroit (which includes Millennials) are from Metro Detroit,[90] and a significant number of the remaining Jewish adults married someone from Metro Detroit. That said, for many years there has been a significant brain drain in Metro Detroit's Jewish community, as Millennials raised in the suburbs overwhelmingly attended state universities in Ann Arbor or East Lansing, and after graduating, moved to New York, Washington DC, Chicago, Los Angeles, San Francisco, or wherever their graduate studies and/or professional pursuits took them in pursuit of a dynamic urban experience.[91]

If you're a Jewish Millennial living in Metro Detroit, there's a good chance that (a) you're from Metro Detroit; (b) you're planning on sticking around because you've decided to stay home (or have already left and decided to return); and (c) some of your closest friends from growing up are no longer living in Metro Detroit.

[89] Priya Parker, *The Art of Gathering* (Penguin, 2018), 38.

[90] Ira Sheskin et al., "2018 Detroit Jewish Population Study." *Jewish Federation of Metropolitan Detroit*, Sep. 2018. www.jewishdatabank.org/content/upload/bjdb/Detroit_2018_Summary_ Report_Jewish_Population_Study.pdf, 14.

[91] Millennials love city living! See, e.g.: Adam Okulicz-Kozaryn and Rubia R. Valente, "No urban malaise for Millennials." *Regional Studies*, 2018. https://www.tandfonline.com/doi/abs/10.1080 /00343404.2018.1453130.

There's also the added advantage of knowing that the people you invest time and energy in befriending are likely to stay local, unlike in some of the country's major cities that attract Millennials.

For example, when my wife and I lived in Washington, DC, there was a couple we were friends with who knew DC would be their long-term home, and who on principle refused to begin new friendships with other couples until they had lived in DC for at least 5 years. They did this because they were so tired of making emotional investments in those who moved away. I'm sure our recruitment efforts for The Well's Shared Interest Groups were helped by participants knowing the relationships being formed had the potential to be long-lasting. That said, the Shared Interest Group model will work regardless of what city you may be in. If your organization is based in a large, comparatively transient city, new arrivals will be looking for ways to make friends, and Shared Interest Groups are a great tool to connect newcomers with one another and your community. When weaving groups together, you can consider the likelihood of individuals residing in that city long-term courtesy of preexisting ties and strive to connect those folks with each other.

As a result of The Well's Shared Interest Groups, roughly 500 Millennials in Metro Detroit got into a rhythm of doing Jewish at least monthly, and we watched friendships blossom. With many people now having 5 friends to do Jewish and life with, we witnessed participation in broader Jewish communal offerings soar. As desired, we were helping to raise the tide for all the community's organizational ships.

The Power of Immersive Experiences

For many years now, we've been aware of the incredible impact of Jewish summer camp. In addition to fostering friendships, identity formation, and embracing Jewish joy, Jewish summer camp participation has a significant positive impact on adult Jewish involvement years later, from practicing rituals, to organizational affiliation, to the embrace of Jewish philanthropy.[92] What's Jewish summer camp's secret sauce? The immersive environment. Camp is a place where Jewish is infused into everything and is the default mode. The noise of the outside world—extracurricular activities, homework, commutes—all fades. The campers and staff can embrace being in a Jewish environment and form intimate bonds with one another. One of the most significant outcomes from immersive experiences like camp is that attendees tend to have a significantly larger proportion of Jewish friends,[93] which as discussed above means a given individual is more likely to actively participate in Jewish life.

Given the outcomes, it's no wonder that the Jewish organizational and philanthropic worlds have been trying to figure out how to harness the power of immersive experiences. But with Millennials as the primary targets, extended experiences aren't a real option. Shorter immersive experiences have been championed as a result. Birthright Israel's trip to Israel lasts 10 days. The American Jewish Joint Distribution Committee's young adult department, known as Entwine, offers weeklong trips to explore Jewish communities and the work of the JDC all over the world. Trybal Gatherings runs adult Jewish summer camp experiences lasting 4-5 days. Honeymoon Israel takes recently married couples on a 9-day trip to Israel. Moishe House offers weekend-long "Learning Retreats" focusing on leadership development, ritual skill acquisition, and Jewish confidence building, and their own 4-day adult Jewish summer camp called Camp Nai Nai Nai.

How long is enough time away to constitute an immersive experience? Based on personal experience as both a participant in and crafter of these experiences, while 24 hours away can be restorative,

---

[92] Steven M. Cohen et al., "Camp Works." *Foundation for Jewish Camp*, 2011. https://jewishcamp.org/campopedia/camp-works-the-long-term-impact-of-jewish-overnight-camp/, 16.
[93] Cohen, 16.

healing and allows for friendships to begin to form, a minimum of 36 hours is required to have an experience fit into an "immersive" construct. Longer durations are ideal but are admittedly more challenging to get Millennials to commit to. The more time spent together as a group, the greater the chance participants will forge friendships that last once they return home.

Speaking of returning home, it's important to know that many of the immersive experiences catering to Jewish Millennials are not location-based. That is, people from all over the world end up on the same trip or experience, and at its conclusion they return to wherever they came from, effectively eliminating the ability to do Jewish locally with one another. Participants on such trips may make some new Jewish friends, but they aren't able to then attend in-person events together due to living in different cities. While there's value in having a network of Jewish friends spread out across the country (especially given the aforementioned Millennial transience), and while technologies have advanced that allow for high quality internet experiences, such as Hadar's Project Zug study buddy platform or sharing Shabbat Dinner via Zoom as so many of us did during the pandemic, day-to-day this is a missed opportunity. It's why city-centric trips, such as those being run by Honeymoon Israel and increasingly JDC Entwine, or Birthright trips run by Hillels for students who are returning to campus, are a more desirable way for these trips to operate if we hope to inspire participants to regularly do Jewish once back home.

For The Well, immersive experiences were a core piece of our community building strategy, as they allowed us to combat Millennial loneliness in real time by bringing folks together while creating environments where people could find their 5 best friends to do Jewish and life with. In addition to annual weekend-long leadership and planning retreats, we hosted "summer camp for young adults" weekends, took multiple group trips to Germany through the Germany

Close Up program, took a group to the Bourbon Trail in Kentucky, organized camping trips in northern Michigan, and more. We also partnered with the Jewish Federation of Metropolitan Detroit on a local Birthright Israel trip, with JDC Entwine on an Israel trip, and with Repair The World on a community service trip to Houston.

Our staff team worked closely with partner organizations and lay leaders to plan and execute each of these experiences. Finding the right lay-leaders to plan with was essential, both due to limited staff bandwidth and their role in recruitment. These experiences also helped us develop a group of super-users who became a kind of Shared Interest Group of their own, with many becoming board members over the years. After each immersive experience, participants returned home together to Metro Detroit with plentiful follow-up opportunities to connect with one another and the broader Jewish community.

What Constitutes Success?

One of the challenges facing the organized Jewish community is that we don't have a shared communal definition as to what constitutes "success." This chapter focuses on the importance of Millennials having Jewish friends, which makes it more likely that they will regularly "do Jewish." But is regular participation in Jewish life sufficient to be considered "success"? Consider this example:

> A Jewish Millennial grows up affiliated with a synagogue. She attends Hebrew School, prepares for and has a Bat Mitzvah, is actively engaged in her youth group during high school, visits Israel, attends Shabbat dinners occasionally at her campus Hillel while in college, and now as an adult is serving on the board of that same synagogue where she grew up. And, when asked, she shares that she is not familiar with

the story of the Binding of Isaac[94] (where God commands Abraham to sacrifice his beloved son Isaac), which in addition to being read annually at services on a designated Saturday morning, is also read each year as part of Rosh Hashanah services.

Is this person a communal success story? Should content knowledge and familiarity with key stories from the Torah matter? Or is success better measured by active participation in community, paying dues to a synagogue and making Federation donations? Is the goal to preserve Judaism? Jewish wisdom? Jewish identity? Jewish culture? Jewish institutions? Repairing the world? Or should the goal be to use these tools to help human beings flourish, as per Rabbi Kula?

Jonathan Mirvis, in his book *It's Our Challenge*, synthesizes these questions (and more) into a model that emphasizes three different approaches for defining Jewish educational success: the literacy approach, the relevancy approach, and the identity/continuity approach.[95] The literacy approach he defines as including mastery both of the Jewish textual tradition, as well as Jewish culture, so that the person can participate in the "great conversations" of Jewish life. The relevancy approach he defines as using Jewish education as a means of enabling individuals to fulfill their personal potential. The identity approach he defines as focusing on facilitating social (and broader) Jewish continuity.[96] All three of these approaches he deems important, recognizing that it's possible for exceptional educational programs to address one, two, or all three approaches in their work.

Another intriguing model developed to help address the "What Constitutes Success?" challenge is the 18x18 Framework, put forth

---

[94] Genesis 22:1-19
[95] Jonathan Mirvis, *It's Our Challenge* (YouCaxton Publications, 2016), 51.
[96] Mirvis, 52.

by Professors Benjamin M. Jacobs and Barry Chazan in partnership with M²: The Institute for Experimental Jewish Education. This model outlines the "18 Jewish things a young Jew should know about, care about, and be able to do by age 18."[97] Mervis's 3 categories are well represented in their list of 18 things. For example, "#3: Have Jewish Friends" would be classified as "identity." "#4: Engage with Jewish role models and personalities" would be classified as "relevancy." "#9: Read and interpret sacred and historical texts and be able to discern Jewish core narratives (stories, sagas, events) and values within them" would be classified as "literacy." I like both models and agree with the need to better articulate communal goals when it comes to how we measure success.

My take is that our overarching goal should be to build Jewish communities that are content-rich, inspiring, meaningful, and relevant. Ones where we help people find friends to do Jewish and life with. Ones that help Jews and those who love them flourish as human beings. As discussed earlier in this chapter, if we want there to be a robust Jewish cultural life—one full of incredible Jewish music, literature, film, theater, language, food, news and more—we need there to be a robust Jewish religious life. Or at the very least, an embrace of models like Shared Interest Groups that provide a regular connection to being, doing and learning Jewish as part of community, and require investment and commitment on the part of the individual. It's up to us to co-create these models with those we're trying to inspire, with a special emphasis on empowering those capable of bringing relational skills, inclusive mindsets, and content knowledge to peer experiences to take on leadership roles.

---

[97] Benjamin M. Jacobs and Barry Chazan. "18x18 Framework." NYU *Applied Research Collective for American Jewry*, 2019. www.ieje.org/wp-content/uploads/2022/05/18x18-Framework-to-use.pdf.

Core Takeaways

1. Embrace each person as an individual and bring intention to helping that person find friends to do Jewish and life with.
2. Make it explicitly clear in your marketing and communications that all are welcome, regardless of whether they happen to be Jewish.
3. Build models where regular participation is expected and where there is some sort of buy-in or reciprocity of commitment. Skin in the game is key!
4. Frequency of participation matters. Consider embracing a goal of monthly participation when it comes to Millennials.
5. Immersive experiences go a long way toward relationship-building and friendship formation. Share immersive experiences with those you're hoping to connect with, and then continue to develop those relationships once back home!

Discussion Questions

- Does our organization bring intention to facilitating Jewish friendships? If so, how so? If not, why not?
- Do our organizational structure and offerings align with a goal of at least monthly participation?
- Does our organization currently use immersive experiences as a relationship-building tool? If so, how can we grow them? If not, why not?
- How does our organization measure success?

chapter 4

"Just Jewish"

*When Pharaoh learned of the matter, he sought
to kill Moses; but Moses fled from Pharaoh.
He arrived in the land of Midian, and sat down beside a well.*
—*Exodus 2:15*

Shortly after graduating from law school, and before beginning my job at a large Metro Detroit law firm, I decided that I needed a car I would feel respectable showing up to client meetings in. After doing some online research, I purchased a used black 2006 Toyota Camry. With a V6 engine, leather interior, moonroof, heated seats and more, it handled beautifully and felt luxurious. It was as close to a Lexus as I could get without buying a Lexus. When I pulled into my friend's driveway to show off the car, his response was, "What if any of your clients work for the Big 3?" My face immediately turned a shade of red, as I realized I'd made a careless mistake.

For many years, Detroit's economy was dominated by America's "Big 3" automakers: Ford, General Motors and Chrysler. A significant number of Detroiters work for the Big 3, work for companies that sell automobiles produced by the Big 3, or work for companies that supply parts to the Big 3. While the percentage of state GDP the automotive industry is responsible for has reduced significantly over the years, Michigan's economy is still quite dependent on the Big 3.[98] Unlike the streets of other major cities, the streets in Metro

---

[98] Rick Haglund, "Michigan's economy is more diverse, but still too dependent on the auto industry." *Michigan Advance,* June 13, 2022. www.michiganadvance.com/2022/06/13/rick-haglund-michigans-economy-is-more-diverse-but-still-too-dependent-on-the-auto-industry/.

Detroit are filled with American-made cars, as Michigan residents are more loyal to American car brands than the residents of any other state.[99] But nationally, the Big 3 don't have the clout they once did, and in 2021, Toyota overtook General Motors for the first time as the top-selling automaker in the United States.[100]

Like the auto industry, much of 20th-century American Judaism was dominated by three major denominations: Reform, Conservative, and Orthodox. Each embracing different approaches to Jewish life and practice, during this time the "Jewish Big 3" became entrenched, building seminaries and networks of synagogues. Far from uniform, within each of the Jewish Big 3, subgroups have evolved (e.g., Classical vs. Mainstream Reform,[101] Modern vs. Ultra Orthodox,[102] etc.). Additional liberal denominations also emerged, with Reconstructing Judaism,[103] Humanistic Judaism, and Jewish Renewal[104] joining the denominational landscape; but none has come close to the size and scale of the Jewish Big 3.

Like the automotive Big 3, the Jewish Big 3 don't have the clout they once did, as "Just Jewish" (or one of its equivalents such as "None" or "No particular branch") is now the most popular answer on surveys when Millennial participants are asked about Jewish denominational affiliation.[105] One might think that those who identify

---

[99] Brandon Champion, "Michigan is more loyal to American car brands than any other state, study says." *MLive*, Oct. 16, 2018. www.mlive.com/news/2018/10/no_state_is_more_loyal_to_amer.html.

[100] Michael Wayland, "Toyota dethrones GM to become America's top-selling automaker in 2021." *CNBC*, Jan. 4, 2022. www.cnbc.com/2022/01/04/toyota-dethrones-gm-to-become-americas-top-selling-automaker-in-2021.html.

[101] Howard A. Berman, "Classical Reform Judaism: What Is It?" 18Doors. www.18doors.org/classical_judaism_a_concise_profile.

[102] Shuli Taubes, "The Delicate Power of Modern Orthodox Judaism." *Harvard Divinity Bulletin*, 2018. www.bulletin.hds.harvard.edu/the-delicate-power-of-modern-orthodox-judaism.

[103] Formerly known as Reconstructionist Judaism.

[104] Jewish Renewal organizationally prefers to describe itself as "transdenominational" or "an attitude." There are many within the Jewish Renewal community, however, who view it as its own denomination. For more: www.aleph.org/what-is-jewish-renewal.

[105] "Jewish Americans in 2020." Pew Research Center, May 11, 2021. www.pewresearch.org/religion/wp-content/uploads/sites/7/2021/05/PF_05.11.21_Jewish.Americans.pdf, 58.

as "Just Jewish" are less likely to be Jewishly engaged than those who identify with a denomination, and for many that may indeed be the case. But Millennials are eschewing labels, with one study finding that Millennials hate labels so much that 60% say they'd rather not be labeled as Millennials![106] As a result, the "Just Jewish" designation includes Millennials of varying Jewish backgrounds, such as those with more traditional religious upbringings and those with few Jewish connections.

To use myself as an example: I was raised in the Conservative Movement, attending both a Conservative synagogue on a weekly basis and a Conservative Movement-affiliated Solomon Schechter Day School. For the past two years I served as a rabbi at a Conservative Synagogue. If I were answering the survey question, I would describe myself as "Just Jewish." There is a vast range of knowledge, experience and practice in the "Just Jewish" category, as many Millennials simply don't want to put themselves into a denominational box.

For some, there is no question that identifying as "Just Jewish" is the result of a lack of education about the Jewish denominations and what their distinct approaches to Judaism are. After all, your average Jew thinks "Orthodox is more, Conservative is medium, Reform is less, and Reconstructionist, what is that?"[107] I can't even begin to tell you how many young adults I've encountered who say they grew up *Reformed*, not actually knowing the proper name of the Reform Movement. Others have said, "I don't do that ritual because I'm super Reform"—as if there is a way to be more or less Reform, or as if the fewer Jewish things one does, the more Reform one is. For some, Reform has (incorrectly) become synonymous with "not practicing or knowledgeable."

---

[106] "Most Millennials Resist the 'Millennial' Label." Pew Research Center, Sep. 3, 2015. www.pewresearch.org/politics/2015/09/03/most-millennials-resist-the-millennial-label.
[107] Terry Bookman, *Beyond Survival* (Rowman & Littlefield, 2019), 131.

With Millennials preferring to avoid labels, is there still value in distinguishing between the denominations? Non-Orthodox denominations are often lumped together as "liberal" Judaism, yet there are significant differences between the Reform, Conservative, Reconstructing, Renewal and Humanistic Jewish denominations, as well as in the practices of those who identify with them.

For illustrative purposes, let's compare those who self-identify as Conservative and those who self-identify as Reform. The Pew Research Center's 2020 study of Jewish Americans found that 69% of Conservative Jews said being Jewish is very important in their lives, while 30% of Reform Jews said the same.[108] While 59% of Conservative-identifying Jews mark Shabbat often or sometimes in a way personally meaningful to them, only 36% of Reform Jews do the same.[109] While 62% of Conservative respondents said that having Jewish grandchildren was important to them, only 29% of Reform respondents said the same.[110] When it comes to interfaith marriage, a much smaller percentage of Conservative Jews intermarry than Reform Jews.[111]

When Moishe House hired an outside firm to conduct their organizational evaluation in 2011, the professionals crafting the survey determined that a Moishe House participant had a "strong Jewish background" if they had at least four of the following six Jewish experiences: 1) Attended a Jewish Day School; 2) Attended or worked at an overnight Jewish camp; 3) Had a Bar/Bat Mitzvah Ceremony; 4) Raised by two Jewish parents; 5) Raised Orthodox or Conservative; and 6) Visited Israel.[112] Built into the research methods was the

---

[108] "Jewish Americans in 2020," 61.
[109] "Jewish Americans in 2020," 73.
[110] "Jewish Americans in 2020," 103.
[111] "Jewish Americans in 2020," 98.
[112] TCC Group, "Evaluation Executive Summary." *Moishe House*, Oct. 1, 2011. www.moishehouse.org/wp-content/uploads/2017/12/EvaluationExecutiveSummary_Revised.pdf, 4.

assumption that being raised in a Conservative Jewish home was an indicator of having a strong Jewish background in a way that being raised in a Reform home was not.

These examples are by no means intended to denigrate the Reform Movement, which has an incredible history of impact and is the largest denomination in the United States today. But there are clearly distinctions between those who identify as Conservative Jews and those who identify as Reform Jews, such that grouping them together in the category of "liberal" as a means of differentiating them from Orthodox Jews doesn't capture the full picture.

There are significant distinctions among the other "liberal" denominations as well. For example, Reconstructing Judaism rejects an interactive God who chose certain people or promised certain lands. Jewish Renewal is neo-Chassidic,[113] embracing the spiritual and mystical, while Humanistic Judaism creates contemporary ritual and embraces the best of Jewish culture, without a belief in God. Each of these denominations has its distinctions which should be championed. Simply grouping them all together as "liberal" shortchanges them all. But will Millennials care?

Chabad

Chabad is a phenomenon in the Jewish world, to put it mildly. Rabbi Menachem Mendel Schneerson (of blessed memory), the seventh and final Lubavitcher Rebbe,[114] sent Jewish emissaries (known as "*shluchim*") to the farthest corners of the world. Comprised of a husband-and-wife team, these couples work to connect with every

---

[113] Neo-Hasidism is an approach by non-Hasidic Jews to spiritually enhance their practice of Judaism by drawing upon the teachings and practices of various Hasidic groups, but without having to conform to their ideology, norms, or Orthodox religious practice.

[114] Chabad, also known as Lubavitch, is an Orthodox Jewish Hasidic dynasty. Rebbe is a Yiddish-German word that connotes a spiritual leader and master of theology in the Hasidic movement. Hasidic Judaism is an Orthodox Jewish religious sect that arose as a spiritual revival movement in the territory of contemporary Western Ukraine during the 18th century.

Jew they can, driven by the principle of *Ahavat Yisrael* (loving every Jew),[115] while modeling a love of God and Torah, and striving to inspire the performance of *mitzvot* and living an Orthodox lifestyle.[116] After the Rebbe's passing, Chabad's leadership decided to double down on sending emissary couples all over the world. At the time of this writing, there are more than 4,900 Chabad emissary families in over 100 countries,[117] and these folks are known for creating welcoming environments that make one feel cared for. I've been graciously hosted for holiday meals at Chabad houses in Thailand, China, and Guatemala. I even lived in an apartment at the Chabad house in Ann Arbor, as it was right down the street from the University of Michigan law school, allowing me to roll out of bed and get to class in under 5 minutes after long nights of "studying." Several Chabad constructs served as inspiration for our work at The Well, and I have tremendous respect for the organization and the work its emissaries do.

Simultaneously, I can't help but be a bit surprised by how ready Millennials are to check their progressive values at the door of their local Chabad house. Jewish Millennials overwhelmingly are in favor of LGBTQ+ equality and marriage,[118] roughly 50% of Jewish Millennials are products of intermarriage themselves,[119] and over 70% will marry someone who doesn't happen to be Jewish. And yet, many are happy to spend time at Chabad, even though Chabad rabbis do not officiate at gay or interfaith weddings, and the movement's definition of who is considered a Jew is significantly narrower than

---

[115] Sue Fishkoff, *The Rebbe's Army* (Schocken Books, 2003), 20.

[116] Fishkoff, 31.

[117] "Fact and Statistics." Chabad. www.chabad.org/library/article_cdo/aid/2346206/jewish/Facts-and-Statistics.htm

[118] "Jewish Americans in 2020," 101.

[119] "Jewish Americans in 2020," 107.

the definition in the Reform and Reconstructing denominations, due to Chabad's rejection of patrilineal descent.[120]

There are a number of other practices and political positions Chabad embraces that would seemingly be problematic for Jewish Millennials, more than 70% of whom identify with or lean toward the (comparatively liberal) Democratic party.[121] For example, the movement endorses the circumcision practice of *metziza b'peh*, where the ritual circumciser (aka *"mohel"*) places his mouth directly on the freshly circumcised baby boy's penis to suck blood from it.[122] Chabad's leadership has advocated for prayer in public schools[123] and doesn't accept the scientific theory of evolution.[124] Embracing messianism, a significant number of Chabad devotees believe wholeheartedly that the late Rebbe Schneerson himself was actually the messiah, and will return to life again.[125] So how is it that politically progressive Millennials are finding themselves hanging out at Chabad?

After over 1,500 coffee dates, what has become clear is this: most simply don't know, and like the child at the Passover Seder, they

---

[120] Traditional Jewish law dictates that one is Jewish if one converts to Judaism or is born to a Jewish mother. The Reconstructionist Movement adopted a resolution in 1968 indicating that it would allow those born to a Jewish father (but not to a Jewish mother) to have equal Jewish status. The Reform Movement followed suit in 1983 (with specific associated requirements as it relates to raising the child exclusively Jewish).

[121] "Jewish Americans in 2020," 160.

[122] This practice dates back over 1,500 years and is explicitly mentioned in the Talmud. Babylonian Talmud, Shabbat, Folio 133a. See also Sharon Otterman. "Denouncing City's Move to Regulate Circumcision." *The New York Times*, Sept. 12, 2012. www.nytimes.com/2012/09/13/nyregion/regulation-of-circumcision-method-divides-some-jews-in-new-york.html.

[123] Menachem M. Schneerson, "Letter on the Question of the Regents Prayer." Nov. 21, 1962. Chabad.org. www.chabad.org/therebbe/letters/default_cdo/aid/1274011/jewish/Non-Denominational-Prayer-in-Public-Schools.htm

[124] Tzvi Freeman, "Does the Theory of Evolution Jibe with Judaism?" *Chabad.org*.www.chabad.org/library/article_cdo/aid/755394/jewish/Does-the-Theory-of-Evolution-Jibe-with-Judaism.htm.

[125] Fishkoff, 270.

don't know how to ask.[126] I had coffee several years ago with a young woman who had recently returned from a Birthright Israel trip. In our conversation, she shared that she had been spending time at Chabad. Given that this young woman was very close friends with a number of folks in the LGBTQ+ community, I asked her how she felt knowing that Chabad rabbis don't officiate at gay weddings, and that the movement has suggested that if you feel same sex attraction, "the best thing for you, for your health, and for your ultimate satisfaction in life is to subdue and re-channel that desire."[127] She was embarrassed to admit that she had no idea that Chabad rabbis would not officiate at gay weddings and that the movement frowned upon homosexuality. Having grown up in a progressive home where *"Tikkun Olam"* ("Repairing the World") was understood to be Judaism's core value, it never crossed her mind to ask what Chabad's position might be.

Many in the Jewish organizational world are afraid of calling attention to or questioning Chabad's worldview, religious practices, and political involvement due to concerns of communal and donor backlash. After all, Chabad is known for welcoming every (matrilineal) Jew regardless of denomination, and the organization's participants and financial supporters around the world are overwhelmingly non-Orthodox Jews.[128] If Jewish organizations criticize Chabad, they're often dismissed as jealous and accused of not "loving all Jews" the way Chabad (incompletely) does. It's a no-win situation. I don't share this information to somehow bash or "other" Chabad. I have been and continue to be inspired by their work. Rather, I think that the "Just Jewish" Millennial embrace of those whose practices

---

[126] It's customary at the Passover Seder to read about 4 different children (wise, wicked, simple, and one who doesn't know how to ask), who serve as pedagogical archetypes in order to provide guidance on how best to teach one's own children about the Exodus from Egypt.

[127] Freeman.

[128] Jack Wertheimer, "Giving Jewish." The AVI CHAI Foundation, 2018. www.avichai.org/wp-content/uploads/2018/03/Giving-Jewish-Jack-Wertheimer.pdf, 24.

and worldviews are fundamentally different than their own bodes quite well for Jewish pluralism.[129]

Jewish Pluralism

Despite very real differences, Jews of all denominations tend to huddle underneath a single organizing umbrella in their respective geographic communities. Usually known as Jewish Federations, these organizations are intentionally pluralistic, charged with caring for the needs of the Jewish people in their local community, in Israel and around the world, regardless of denomination. I find Jewish pluralism both valuable and challenging. On the one hand, it makes sense for us to band together, if for no reason other than the comparatively small size of the Jewish population. Antisemites don't distinguish between types of Jews,[130] so there's value in us sticking together despite our differences. And yet, when it comes to appreciating Jewish practice and observance in its various expressions, it's often those on the more liberal end of the spectrum who are pluralistic, while many Orthodox Jews are not.

Rabbi Avi Shafran, chief spokesperson for Agudath Israel of America (the main organization representing America's Haredi[131] Jews), wrote the following in the *Times of Israel* in July of 2022:

> Our deeply held principles do not allow us to accept Jewish theologies that reject essential elements of the millennia-old Jewish *mesorah,* or religious tradition, that lies at the root of each and every Jew. And so, we must reject all theologies that, sadly, have jettisoned the Jewish *mesorah.* My wife and I raised our children

---

[129] For a fascinating deep dive on Jewish Pluralism and its evolution, check out this article: Yehuda Kurtzer. "What Happened to Jewish Pluralism?" *Sources: A Journal of Jewish Ideas,* Spring 2021. www.sourcesjournal.org/articles/what-happened-to-jewish-pluralism.

[130] "Antisemitism." Yad Vashem. www.yadvashem.org/odot_pdf/Microsoft%20Word%20-%205742.pdf

[131] Haredi (or "ultra-Orthodox") Judaism refers to groups within Orthodox Judaism that are characterized by their strict adherence to Jewish law, and who reject modern values and practices.

(who are today raising their own the very same way) and I have taught hundreds of students over decades, to understand that only fealty to the Torah—as it has been understood and observed over the centuries and in the face of terrible challenges—can legitimately be called Judaism.[132]

For Haredi Jews, Jewish denominational expressions other than Orthodoxy are not Judaism. We can preach pluralism all we want, but we must acknowledge that a significant and growing portion of the Jewish world simply isn't interested.[133] No one would ever expect Catholic and Protestant institutions to exist under the same "Christian Federation" umbrella, or to see a communal fundraising apparatus soliciting Protestant dollars in order to fund Catholic schools or vice versa. And yet, we see Jewish Federations supporting "LGBTQ Pride" and "Interfaith Couples" affinity groups on the one hand, and ultra-Orthodox day schools, where those life realities are rejected, on the other. In an era where people like to personalize their philanthropy rather than give to umbrella organizations and would not want to be seen supporting causes that preach values anathema to their own, I'm not surprised many of our Federations have struggled with attracting Millennial donors to their annual campaigns.

That said, as evidenced by how many are happy to spend time with Chabad, Jewish Millennials clearly have the potential to be pluralistic in their outlook and to appreciate the centralized role of Federations as a result. Judaism has historically been counter-cul-

---

[132] Avi Shafran, "No tolerance for hooliganism." *Times of Israel*, July 12, 2022. https://blogs.timesofisrael.com/no-tolerance-for-hooliganism

[133] Orthodox Jews have significantly higher birthrates than those of other (or no) denominations, leading to significant growth within the denomination, and making up an increasing share of the Jewish community overall. "Jewish Americans in 2020." Pew Research Center, May 11, 2021. www.pewresearch.org/religion/wp-content/uploads/sites/7/2021/05/PF_05.11.21_Jewish.Americans.pdf, 188.

tural, and the idea that in our polarized and hyper-partisan historical moment that Jews are supporting one another even when they see the world quite differently is powerful. "Unity but not uniformity" is the rallying cry our Federations need to amplify going forward.

Building a B-Brand

With Jewish denominational labels being rejected by Millennials while simultaneously being embraced and valued by their parents and grandparents, what are our denominationally affiliated organizations to do?

Growing up in Metro Detroit, it was a frequent occurrence to hear those in older generations reminisce about the good old days, when they would go into the city to shop at Hudson's. This monstrosity of a department store occupied an entire city block, and for many years, at 25 stories tall, was the tallest retail building in the world.[134] Founded in 1881, the store thrived until the 1960s, when many of its customers moved to the suburbs. As Downtown Detroit declined as a popular destination for both living and shopping, Hudson's, which was formally known as the J.L. Hudson Co., merged into the department store division of the Dayton-Hudson Corp, which ultimately decided to eliminate the Hudson's brand from the marketplace.

What most folks don't know or realize is that the Dayton-Hudson Corp. made the decision to wind down that part of its business portfolio largely courtesy of having built an incredibly successful B-Brand, known as Target. Target became so successful that in 2000 the Dayton-Hudson Corp. changed its name to Target Corporation. As of this writing, if you visit Daytons.com and Hudsons.com, they both automatically redirect you to Target.com.

What is a B-Brand? Large companies often create secondary brands, known as B-Brands, that they use to explore market trends

---

[134] "Hudson's Site." Bedrock Management Services, 2023. www.hudsonssitedetroit.com/history/.

or to try to wrestle back market share from lower priced competitors. For example, Coca-Cola rolled out a new soft drink brand in India in 2017 called "Kinley Flavors" at a significantly lower price than traditional Coke as a means of trying to capture the lower end of the market which was dominated by competitors.[135] While the Dayton-Hudson Corp. was running its flagship department stores, it simultaneously built Target, a lower-cost retailer that could help identify consumer trends, and which ultimately ended up being more valuable than the core department store business itself.

It is well documented that Millennials in general aren't fans of institutions—religious or secular.[136] If we were to build an effective Jewish Millennial engagement initiative in an era of "Just Jewish," we knew we couldn't lead with Temple Israel's name or logo, as it would likely do more harm than good. We could anticipate potential responses to outreach such as "Oh, you're part of Temple Israel? Well, I grew up at a different synagogue, so no thanks." Or, "Oh, you're part of Temple Israel? Your goal must be to get me to join your synagogue and I'm not interested."

This was hard for Temple Israel's leadership to hear. After all, for those seeking synagogue life, Temple Israel's brand and reputation were excellent. You don't become the largest synagogue in the country without folks appreciating your brand. And if you've chosen to be part of the Temple's leadership, you clearly care deeply about the institution, and are likely to have been positively impacted by your association with it.

After many conversations, it was the framing of Dayton-Hudson Corp. and Target that helped Temple Israel's leadership understand the value of building a B-Brand. There certainly was no expectation

---

[135] "Coca-Cola takes on B brands." *WARC*, Nov. 7, 2017. www.warc.com/newsandopinion/news/coca-cola-takes-on-%27b-brands%27/38953.

[136] David Masci, "Q&A: Why Millennials are less religious than older Americans." Pew Research Center, Jan. 8, 2016. www.pewresearch.org/fact-tank/2016/01/08/qa-why-millennials-are-less-religious-than-older-americans.

that The Well would grow such that it would surpass Temple Israel—especially since on principle The Well never offered Hebrew School, High Holiday or Bar/Bat/B-Mitzvah services, due to the desire to inspire Millennials to one day affiliate with synagogues and other community organizations. Rather, The Well was going to disrupt the local Millennial engagement marketplace by adding a distinctly inclusive Jewish voice to it, identifying relevant trends along the way. We were charged with raising the tide for all the community's organizational ships by increasing the number of connected, engaged and passionate Millennial Jews in Metro Detroit.

Several Jewish organizations have inserted B-Brands into the marketplace, each with different structures and relationships to the parent entity. Many, like the Jewish Renaissance Project (Penn Hillel), The Riverway Project (Temple Israel of Boston), and the Soul Center (Beth El Congregation in Baltimore), have found success. The Well's structure was unique as compared with these and most other Jewish communal B-Brands in two key ways: First, while I was accountable to Temple Israel's leadership in that they had the ability to fire me, they were not involved in the day-to-day operations or decision-making processes of The Well in any way. Second, I had no work responsibilities for Temple Israel—my efforts were reserved exclusively for The Well. Despite these realities, there were community members, rabbis, and potential funders who struggled to understand the construct and perceived The Well as Temple Israel operating "in disguise."

Naming Our B-Brand

What considerations went into picking a name for our new B-Brand, and how did we ultimately choose the name "The Well"? Our goal was to reach folks who wouldn't ordinarily make Jewish choices. So, while we considered Hebrew names for the organization, such as *Hamakom* ("The Place"), *Gesher* ("The Bridge"), and *Achla* ("Awesome"), we decided that those might alienate folks, feeling "too Jewish" for some members of our target audience. While thinking about a web domain, Hebrew words had the potential for transliteration misspellings that might frustrate someone trying to reach our website. In the end, it was my wife Miriam who suggested that we go with "The Well," which felt fitting considering that in the Jewish tradition the prophetess Miriam is associated with water:

> The Israelites arrived at the wilderness of Zin on the first new moon, and the people stayed at Kadesh. Miriam died there and was buried there. The community was without water, and they congregated against Moses and Aaron.[137]

The famous Torah commentator Rashi[138] taught that since the statement about the community lacking water came immediately after mentioning Miriam's death, we can infer that during the 40 years the Israelites wandered in the desert, the mystical well of water that accompanied them existed thanks to Miriam's merit.[139] Essentially, Miriam and water—and wells specifically—have a special place in the Jewish tradition. So, when my wife Miriam suggested the name The Well, it seemed an appropriate fit!

When you read the Torah, you find that most of the cool things that happened in its narratives happened at the well. In ancient Middle Eastern culture, the well was not only where you drew water. It was the local coffee shop, singles bar, office water cooler, and more! When you visited the biblical well, you were nourished and you often took something away with you when you left—both goals we aspired to achieve when people visited The Well. Simply put, the

---

[137] Numbers 20:1-2
[138] "Rashi" is an acronym for renowned medieval French Torah commentator **Rabbi Shlomo Itzchaki** (1040-1105 CE).
[139] Babylonian Talmud, Taanit, Folio 9a.

biblical well is where people gathered, and we wanted our modern iteration of The Well to be a place where Metro Detroit's Jewish Millennials would regularly gather!

One of the early challenges we faced when trying to differentiate our brand from others in the marketplace related to language choices. Did we want to self-describe as Pluralistic? Liberal? Progressive? Inclusive?

We're living during a time of intense political polarization. While words like "liberal" and "progressive" need not have specifically political meanings, they do in contemporary American discourse. "Liberal" and "Progressive" are names often ascribed to the Reform Movement outside of America.[140] But when considering both of those words, we decided quickly that our American realities wouldn't allow for us to use those words, fearing that being perceived as an overtly political organization would both dissuade Millennials with conservative leanings from participating and scare away potential donors. We also wanted to define ourselves by what we were rather than what we weren't, so "non-Orthodox" wasn't going to work. In some of our earliest website language and grant applications, we went with the term "pluralistic." Aside from being a buzzword associated with any given number of Jewish organizations, we figured it was a term familiar to both Millennials and potential donors, indicating an openness to all.

In addition to the challenges of pluralism expressed earlier in this chapter, another significant challenge is that when cultivating pluralistic spaces, where everyone's unique needs are considered, organizations often end up having no choice but to cater to the "*frummest*[141] common denominator." In other words, to have Orthodox Jews feel welcome, Orthodox religious restrictions need to be embraced as

---

[140] For example, see: "Affirmations of Liberal Judaism." Union of Liberal and Progressive Synagogues, 2017. www.liberaljudaism.org/wp-content/uploads/2020/03/Affirmations-of-Liberal-Judaism-Booklet-MAR-2020.pdf.

[141] *Frum* is a Yiddish word that means pious.

it relates to food, where and when gatherings take place, whether women are permitted to sing at said gatherings, and more. Given that The Well had been created to serve as a counterpoint to the myriad Orthodox-affiliated outreach groups seeking to engage Millennials, and that we were unashamedly going to gather on Shabbat, have prayer services using musical instruments and women's voices, serve vegetarian food from restaurants lacking formal kosher certification and more, we realized that "pluralistic" wasn't really the right word to describe the organization.

After soliciting feedback from some of our early participants, we transitioned away from using the word "pluralistic," landing instead on the word "inclusive." We wanted to make it clear that as an organization we embraced interfaith couples, LGBTQ+ folks, etc. Yet we knew that using the word inclusive might also be problematic.

There's a classic South Park episode that plays on Holocaust imagery where the main characters, accused of being intolerant of others, are sent to "The Death Camp of Tolerance."[142] There, they are forced by an SS-like officer to create finger paintings of children of mixed races holding hands, while the officer bellows at them: "We will not tolerate intolerance!" (Which of course means he's being intolerant—of those he deems to be intolerant.)

We recognized that the word "inclusive" has its own shortcomings, as we were not inclusive of those we perceived as being exclusive. That is, we were inclusive of those who shared our vision of inclusion, which means we weren't entirely inclusive. But we embraced the word and were pleased to learn that for several of our interfaith couples, the word "inclusive" is a signaling word they look for when trying to determine whether a Jewish organization will warmly welcome them. We updated our language, and began referring to The Well as "An *inclusive* Jewish community building, education and spirituality initiative."

---

[142] *South Park*, Season 6, Episode 14.

Using Third Places

From the very beginning, there were conversations about whether The Well should have its own physical programming space. After all, a key way that B-Brands tend to distinguish themselves from their parent companies is by having their own storefronts. One of the running jokes in Jewish life is that the organizations who have buildings often wish they didn't due to the costs associated with maintaining them, while those without buildings often wish they had their own dedicated spaces. There's something to be said about not having to *shlep* supplies all over town every time you host a gathering! As referenced earlier, according to legend, Miriam's Well moved with the people as they wandered through the desert. As a result, we decided that at least initially, we were going to be a portable organization, using various Third Places for our gatherings.

What's a Third Place? The term was coined by sociologist Ray Oldenburg and refers to places where people spend time between home ("first" place) and work ("second" place).[143] For some, synagogues and/or JCCs serve as Third Places. For most Millennials, they don't (yet!). Rather than trying to attract Millennials to a distinctly Jewish Third Place, we chose to position ourselves out in the community in the places our target demographic was already frequenting, such as coffee shops, bowling alleys, restaurants, and public parks. If there was a trendy spot in town, we wanted to be there, meeting people in the places they frequented or wanted to explore.

Using Third Places also allowed us to bring intention to selecting venues that would best allow us to accomplish our goals. Author Priya Parker emphasizes in her book *The Art of Gathering* the value of starting planning by framing the end goals for a particular gathering and working backwards to determine the various ingredients that will allow for those goals to be achieved—including selecting a

---

[143] Stuart M. Butler and Carmen Diaz, "'Third places' as community builders." Brookings, Sep. 14, 2016. www.brookings.edu/blog/up-front/2016/09/14/third-places-as-community-builders

venue that will embody the reason for your convening.[144] We didn't have the option to host gatherings in our own building because we didn't have one, so we embraced Parker's method. A few years into The Well's work, we were approached by a donor willing to provide us with a space of our own. But when the donor learned that we would continue using various Third Places around town to make sure that our venue selection aligned with our goals for particular gatherings, and that we wouldn't commit to hosting all of our gatherings in the space, they backed away.

B-Brand Fundraising Challenges

While using a B-Brand was the right decision as it related to accomplishing The Well's outreach and engagement goals, it admittedly created some fundraising challenges. The Well was not incorporated as an independent 501c3. Instead, Temple Israel served as The Well's fiscal sponsor, which allowed us to have charitable tax status for donation purposes. Many potential donors perceived Temple Israel, with an operating budget north of $8 million at the time, as being flush with cash, and would question why we needed $10,000 here and $40,000 there for The Well when Temple Israel theoretically could have funded us themselves. Many foundations said that it was not their practice to fund synagogue programs; their concern was that if they funded one synagogue program, they'd have to fund all of them. My impression is that many funders didn't see synagogues as capable of innovating, and assumed that if they did it'd only be to the benefit of their existing membership as opposed to benefitting the broader community. These kinds of concerns were brought up so frequently from potential funders—especially those who required audited financial statements, to whom I had to submit the book-length volumes of Temple Israel's audited financials—that I drafted a 1-page explanation document laying out the relationship between Temple Israel and The Well that I'd submit with grant applications.

[144] Priya Parker, *The Art of Gathering* (Penguin, 2018), 55.

What is the relationship between The Well and Temple Israel?

The Well is a project of the Lori Talsky Fund at Temple Israel.

Lori Talsky (who is not herself a member of Temple Israel), is The Well's pilot donor. The pilot investment, along with all additional dollars raised by The Well, is kept in a separate, distinct fund, which solely supports The Well—a project created specifically to benefit the Metro Detroit Jewish community broadly.

Temple Israel serves as The Well's fiscal sponsor (allowing for The Well to have 501c3 charitable status), and provides in-kind support by handling The Well's back office work (such as payroll and accounting), and by making its resources such as tables, chairs, audio/visual equipment, etc. available for The Well to borrow at no cost when available.

Temple Israel does not allocate any dollars to The Well from their organizational budget. So too, Temple Israel does not charge The Well for the back-end support it provides.

The Well's professional team are technically employees of Temple Israel due to the Fund being housed there, but they have zero Temple Israel-related responsibilities, work off-site, and have complete independence in creating and scheduling The Well's programming.

Temple Israel does not have any expectations as it relates to "recruiting" those The Well touches to join Temple Israel specifically. The goal of The Well is to inspire Millennial Jewish connectivity and commitment in Metro Detroit broadly, to the ultimate benefit of all of the community's institutions (including synagogues, JCCs, camps, Federation & agencies, etc.).

Clarifying the fiscal relationship between The Well and Temple Israel proved valuable for several funders. Others, however, couldn't get past the relationship and avoided investing in our work. Most importantly, most of the Millennials we engaged had no idea about the relationship and embraced The Well as an independent brand. For a "Just Jewish" generation, the B-Brand approach was a clear success.

Core Takeaways

1. Avoid leading with denominational labels during the relationship-building phase with Millennials. Rather, focus on building genuine relationships, and along the way make clear what your institution stands for and values.
2. "Unity but not Uniformity" is a pluralistic rallying cry that will speak to Millennials.
3. To better reach Millennials, consider piloting a B-Brand. Embrace its ability to disrupt your local market while identifying trends. Be thoughtful when naming it.
4. Language matters! Bring intention to the words you use to describe your organization and be aware that certain words serve as indicators for various historically marginalized groups as they try to determine whether they'll be welcomed.
5. Even if your ultimate goal is to get people to come to and feel comfortable in your building, you must be ready and willing to go and meet the people where they are first. It is through relationships of trust forged outside of your building that Millennials will be willing to cross the threshold into it.
6. The guiding question can't be "How do I get Millennials to pay membership dues at my institution?" Rather, it needs to be, "How are we building deep relationships and using Judaism to help transform lives?" Everything else will flow from there.

Discussion Questions

- What is our organizational brand? How should it change, if at all, in a "Just Jewish" moment?
- If we were to take out a full-page newspaper ad (either digital or print) in the *New York Times* to promote our organization, what would it look like and say?
- What differentiates us from other organizations in the marketplace?
- How does our organization learn about emerging market trends?
- If our organization were to create a B-Brand, what would its purpose and focus be?
- Is our organization choosing venues for gatherings that best help us meet our goals? Why or why not?

chapter 5

How *Field of Dreams* Got It Wrong

And let them make Me a sanctuary that
I may dwell among them.
—Exodus 25:8

One of the most important movies of my childhood was *Field of Dreams*. Based on W. P. Kinsella's 1982 novel *Shoeless Joe*, this baseball-centered classic (made in 1989), starring Kevin Costner, James Earl Jones, Ray Liotta and others, captured the lore, mystique and majesty of America's Pastime better than any other movie ever had. Costner's character is a farmer in Iowa who, after hearing whispers offering instructions, builds a baseball field in his cornfield that attracts the ghosts of baseball legends, including Shoeless Joe Jackson and the infamous Chicago Black Sox who were accused of throwing the 1919 World Series. At the end, Costner's character encounters the young ghost of his late father, and they then have a catch together. Cue the waterworks! The most famous "whisper" from the film is the one that inspires Costner's character to build the baseball field in the first place: "If you build it, he will come."

This mantra has been the driving ethos of much of 20th- and 21st-century American Jewish life. "If we made the prayer services shorter, more people would come." "If we remodeled the social hall, more people would come." "If we had top of the line tennis court lights for night play, more people would come." "If we did 'x,' more people would come" has been a rallying cry for the Jewish community for quite some time.

And yet, with all due respect to the whispering ghost in *Field of Dreams*, "If you build it, they will come" is not the rallying cry for Jewish Millennials. Instead, it's "If you empower them to build it with you, they will come, and will also invite their friends." Not as succinct or catchy (maybe it would be if James Earl Jones recorded it), but true. The core distinction is between building something "for you," and building something "with you."

Millennials are accustomed to customizing offerings for themselves and don't have any particular loyalty to the institution providing the goods or services. Rabbi Kerry Olitzky explains this mindset in his book *Playlist Judaism*, pointing to internet music company Napster fundamentally changing the way people consume music as the root cause. While in the past people had relied on experts to curate musical selections and the order they were played in or bought an entire CD just to listen to a single song, thanks to Napster people were able to pick which specific songs they wanted to listen to and in what order, without having to buy albums or rely on the expertise of disc jockeys.[145] This thoroughly disrupted the music business, and personal customization has been the expectation ever since.

We see this playing out in many areas of contemporary life. For example, notice the large number of fast-casual restaurants that are set up like cafeteria lines where you select what you want from an assortment of plentiful ingredients. Whether the cuisine of choice is pizza, poke bowls, burritos, or salads, Millennials want to help craft experiences that are unique to their tastes and not just consume what's "built" for them without their input. Not interested in being passive consumers, Millennials want to feel they are part of a co-creative process, with a hand in designing the experiences they partake in.

This is a challenge for Legacy Organizations, many of which are accustomed to a more "top-down" approach with budgets that de-

---

[145] Kerry M. Olitzky, *Playlist Judaism* (Rowman & Littlefield, 2013), 8.

pend on institutional loyalty. In the synagogue world, it's common to hear complaints that families only join—if at all—when it's time for Hebrew School to begin for their eldest child, and then discontinue their membership when their youngest child has concluded their Bar/Bat/B-Mitzvah. In an era when Jewish Millennials are marrying later and having fewer children,[146] the synagogue membership window for many is significantly shorter than it was in prior generations, impacting synagogue bottom lines.[147]

Feeling that anything short of a lifetime commitment constitutes failure makes the Jewish organizational world an outlier as well. In the private sector, if I told a small business owner that she could acquire a new customer today who'd remain a loyal customer for the next 8 years, she'd likely jump up and down with excitement and gratitude. In the Jewish world, if I told a synagogue they could welcome a new family who'd be loyal customers for 8 years, the response would more likely be: "but what about the other 112 years?"[148] I don't fault our organizations for wanting relationships that last a lifetime and go beyond a consumer model. I agree that's ideal. Relationships are everything, and the way to build deep, authentic relationships with Millennials is to treat them as co-creative partners as opposed to consumers, pivoting into an Empowerment-Centric Co-Creation model.

Empowerment-Centric Co-Creation

What do I mean by "Empowerment-Centric Co-Creation"? First, if you're not familiar with the phrase, it's okay—I made it up! Es-

---

[146] Sylvia Barack Fishman and Steven M. Cohen, "Family, Engagement, and Jewish Continuity among American Jews." The Jewish People Policy Institute, 2017. www.jppi.org.il/wp-content/uploads/2017/06/Raising-Jewish-Children-Research-and-Indicators-for-Intervention.pdf, 7.

[147] Stephen Windmueller, "Mergers and More: What Is Happening to the American Synagogue, and Why?" *Jewish Journal*, Nov. 12, 2020. www.jewishjournal.com/commentary/324722/mergers-and-more-what-is-happening-to-the-american-synagogue-and-why.

[148] Moses died at 120, and our tradition suggests that 120 is thus an aspirational number of years to live. On people's birthdays, it's common to say *"ad me'ah v'esrim!"* – "[may you live] until 120!"

sentially, to use an Empowerment-Centric Co-Creation approach means that from the very beginning of a gathering's planning stages, members of the target group are invited to be co-creators with the professional team in designing and executing the gathering and are empowered to share their ideas and feel ownership over it. By no means am I suggesting that we were somehow pioneers at The Well on this front, as there are many organizations that use similar co-creation methods. We just came up with a fun new name for it and made it a core component of our programmatic philosophy! The Well engaged hundreds of Millennials each year in a co-creative process (and thousands more who participated in the co-created offerings) using the Empowerment-Centric Co-Creation model.

The Empowerment-Centric Co-Creation model has 10 steps:

1. Identify those you want to invite into the co-creative process.
2. Extend a personal invitation to each of those people (and/or organizations) at least three months in advance of the gathering's target date.
3. Emphasize that co-creating together is a big deal, and how much you value their input.
4. Assemble the group at least monthly, with regular communication between meetings.
5. At the first meeting, brainstorm together. Keep an open mind. Ask open ended questions and be willing to explore ideas you never would have considered yourself.
6. As you refine the ideas, make it clear that time is of the essence, creating a sense of urgency-based creativity. Also, share any other limitations that might exist, such as budget, dietary restrictions, etc.
7. Together, concretize a vision for the gathering.

8. Distribute tasks among the group, empowering co-creators to take on substantive tasks.
9. Execute the gathering!
10. Be sure to raise up and express gratitude to your co-creators at the gathering itself, emphasizing the important role they played in making it happen.

The Empowerment-Centric Co-Creation model has a key weakness: it takes significantly more staff bandwidth to implement than planning and executing programs alone. Planning and executing a program alone is easy when compared with co-creating, where extra steps are taken to empower emerging leaders. I'm not surprised that many organizations hire "Program Directors" whose job is to create programs that they then try to attract people to because it's easier, cheaper and, at first glance, takes less time. But the classic Program Director role, absent an embrace of co-creation, is the epitome of "If you build it, they will come."

Pain Points

There are three key reasons Jewish Millennials don't take on leadership roles in the Jewish community, each of which needs to be addressed when inviting them into a process of co-creation: (1) perceived lack of time, (2) perceived lack of dollars, and (3) lack of confidence, specifically as it relates to facilitating Jewish ritual.[149]

(Perceived) Lack of Time

It should come as no surprise that many view time as their most valuable commodity. Judaism embraces this viewpoint, sanctify-

---

[149] I first became aware of this framing when attending the Re:Kindle conference in January of 2016 hosted by The Leichtag Foundation and The Charles and Lynn Schusterman Family Philanthropies, where OneTable presented the findings of their market research conducted by consultant Jamie Betesh Carter.

ing time weekly (Shabbat!). Time is something you can't get back once it has been lost. There are even studies that show that happiness increases when you're able to hire out tasks (such as cooking, cleaning, and grocery shopping) to others to create additional time for yourself.[150]

Despite what you may have heard, Millennials are working long hours,[151] and are now hyper-connected to work courtesy of technologies that keep them on-call 24/7.[152] Yet we know that people make time for the things they're invested in. Many Jewish Millennials make time for exercise, brunch with friends, time with family, watching Netflix, volunteering, and more. Simply put, if you can get Jewish Millennials excited about and invested in a project, the time often will magically appear. As author Daniel Pink might put it, if we inspire them with Purpose,[153] they'll make the time.

As discussed in Chapter 1, it's important to remember that Millennials fall into three distinct life stages: Singles, Couples, and Parents. Once people become parents, their available time is significantly reduced, as it becomes devoted overwhelmingly to the project of parenting. This is particularly true when children are young and require constant attention and support. The result is that empowering and co-creating with the Millennial parents of young children is much more challenging than when working with those who don't have children.

---

[150] Ashley V. Whillans et al., "Buying time promotes happiness." *PNAS*, vol. 114, no. 32, July 2017. www.pnas.org/doi/full/10.1073/pnas.1706541114#ref-3.

[151] Sarah Green Carmichael, "Millennials Are Actually Workaholics, According to Research." *Harvard Business Review*, Aug. 17, 2016. www.hbr.org/2016/08/millennials-are-actually-workaholics-according-to-research.

[152] This is so prevalent that there are some countries now outlawing employers contacting employees after work hours. See, e.g., Bryan Robinson, "It's Becoming Illegal If Employers Contact Employees After Work, New Research Shows." *Forbes*, Mar. 1, 2022. www.forbes.com/sites/bryanrobinson/2022/03/01/its-becoming-illegal-if-employers-contact-employees-after-work-new-research-shows.

[153] Daniel H. Pink, *Drive* (Riverhead Books, 2011), 133.

Since in the Empowerment-Centric Co-Creation model there are professional staff who are part of the co-creation process and are there to help bring the vision of lay leaders to fruition, we were able to effectively eliminate concerns about time. Even if a lay leader couldn't execute their great idea or lean into the process entirely due to time constraints, we had professional staff at The Well who could step in and help execute their vision. This was exciting and attractive to Millennials in all three stages of life, who eagerly entered into co-creative partnerships with us.

(Perceived) Lack of Dollars

Many Millennials entered the workforce (or attempted to) during The Great Recession, the economic downturn from 2007-2009 that came about because of the bursting of the U.S. housing bubble and accompanying global financial crisis. It took many years for the economy to recover. Along with skyrocketing costs for college and graduate school, student loans and other debt, later marriage and lower rates of homeownership, and then the global pandemic, it's no surprise that many are concerned about Millennials and their financial well-being, with headlines such as "Millennials Are Running Out Of Time To Build Wealth" common.[154] Many have monthly student loan payment obligations which function as a second rent or mortgage payment, reducing disposable income in a way that was not the case for previous generations. It might surprise you to learn that Millennials are saving more for retirement than previous generations did—likely because of having lived through the traumas of The Great Recession and Covid, and witnessing America's crumbling safety net. Many Millennials are concerned about retirement, with more than 70% pessimistic about achieving financial

---

[154] Olivia Rockeman and Catarina Saraiva, "Millennials Are Running Out of Time to Build Wealth." *Bloomberg*, June 3, 2021. www.bloomberg.com/features/2021-millennials-are-running-out-of-time.

security.[155] While they may enjoy splurging on avocado toast here and there, general Millennial sentiments related to finances often includes stress, concern, and insecurity.

To be fair, using economic data for Millennials broadly may not be the best dataset to use when considering Jewish Millennials specifically, because "as a whole, U.S. Jews are a relatively high-income group, with roughly half saying their annual household income is at least $100,000—much higher than the percentage of all U.S. households at that level."[156] U.S. Jews are more affluent than the average American, implying that Jewish Millennials likely have more disposable income to spend than average American Millennials, or at the very least may not have to save as intentionally, as they are more likely to benefit via inheritance in the future.[157] My impression is that even those who are financially secure and don't have student debt are worried about finances and also feel these same sentiments of stress, concern and insecurity. Let's not forget that more than 25% of U.S. Jews say that they have recently had difficulty paying for medical care, rent, mortgage, food, or other bills or debts.[158] Given these realities, the notion that a Jewish Millennial is going to pay for something they aren't regularly using is unlikely.

In the Empower-Centric Co-Creation model, membership constructs and dollars weren't part of the conversation at all. We sought to empower Jewish Millennials—regardless of membership or affiliation status—to feel ownership and excitement over building something Jewish for themselves and others. We had an organizational programming budget to help make their visions come to life at no

---

[155] Nicole Goodkind, "Millennials are ahead of their parents in retirement savings." *CNN Business*, Apr. 27, 2022. www.cnn.com/2022/04/27/investing/retirement-millennials-boomers-saving-more/index.html.

[156] "Economics and well-being among U.S. Jews." Pew Research Center, May 11, 2021. www.pewresearch.org/religion/2021/05/11/economics-and-well-being-among-u-s-jews.

[157] Eric Levitz, "Will 'the Great Wealth Transfer' Trigger a Millennial Civil War?" *New York Magazine*, July 18, 2021. www.nymag.com/intelligencer/2021/07/will-the-great-wealth-transfer-spark-a-millennial-civil-war.html.

[158] "Economics and well-being among U.S. Jews." Pew Research Center, May 11, 2021.

cost to them, and to help make attendance affordable via subsidies when necessary. We were seeking investments of time and talent more than treasure at this stage of the relationship. Lack of dollars was simply not an excuse not to participate! When it came time to invite the community to invest in our work, those we had engaged in the co-creative process were much more likely to donate than the average participant, and they contributed larger dollar amounts, too.

Lack of Confidence

In addition to concerns about time and dollars, the third leg of the "why aren't Jewish Millennials doing Jewish more often" stool is a lack of confidence as it relates to ritual facilitation. Millennial Jewish gatherings skew social, often lacking substantive Jewish content. For example, Moishe House's 2015 organizational evaluation showed that social gatherings are offered across their network more often than any other type of gathering and have the highest attendance rates.[159] This is because many Jewish Millennials are self-conscious about how little they know when it comes to facilitating Jewish ritual experiences for others. As Rabbi Sid Schwarz writes in *Finding a Spiritual Home*, "Jews who are well educated and professionally successful come to feel uneasy when they are put into a setting that makes them feel incompetent."[160] Hosting a Shabbat dinner for friends seems daunting if you're worried people are going to judge you for not knowing the blessings that accompany the rituals.

For anyone reading who is surprised that Jewish Millennials might be intimidated by offering a few one-line blessings to begin a Shabbat dinner, a friend recently shared with me a story about a young leadership trip he took overseas with a prominent Jewish organization. The group was visiting with the local community, and

---

[159] "Moishe House: 2015 Evaluation Findings Executive Summary." *Informing Change*. Moishe House, Apr. 2015. www.moishehouse.org/wp-content/uploads/2017/12/mh_2015_eval.pdf, 3.

[160] Sidney Schwarz, *Finding a Spiritual Home* (Jewish Lights, 2003), 252.

at a large-scale Shabbat dinner for both natives and visitors, the lay chair of the young leadership group was invited to offer the *Hamotzi* blessing over challah to initiate the Shabbat meal. He did not know the one-line blessing and was embarrassed to have to admit it in front of his peers. Many of those who comprise our community's future leadership don't have basic building blocks when it comes to Jewish education. And lest you think I'm somehow picking on those lacking formal Jewish educations, even those who grew up going to Jewish Day School can be self-conscious about ritual skill facilitation as adults, with many having not led them for years, and/or not having had them modeled at home as children.

During my time as the organizational rabbi at Moishe House, we addressed this reality by crafting immersive learning experiences, which generally took the form of weekend-long retreats at various summer camps around the country (and later, the world). Each weekend retreat had a theme, such as "How to do Shabbat," "How to do Sukkot," or "How to do Passover," where we did all we could to educate, inspire and empower attendees to return home and facilitate Shabbat and holiday experiences for their peers. The solution to a lack of literacy and confidence is not avoiding Jewish content or dumbing it down, but rather providing supportive spaces to teach and empower folks in those components of Jewish life!

One of the perks of The Well's Empowerment-Centric Co-Creation model is the ability to identify confidence pain points with co-creators in advance and to make the time to teach, coach and mentor them, so that they can confidently curate experiences for others. In addition, at larger-scale gatherings, the opportunity existed for ritual facilitation to fall on the staff team's shoulders, meaning our co-creators didn't have to stress facilitating rituals if they didn't want to, though they were always encouraged to try. In that way, we were able to eliminate concerns relating to confidence.

What's special about the Empowerment-Centric Co-Creation model is that if done well, those you've engaged in the co-creative process are so excited about what they're creating with you that they serve as ambassadors for the gathering and invite their peers to attend, eliminating a significant amount of time that would otherwise be spent on marketing and recruitment. As discussed earlier, there is nothing more likely to pull a Jewish Millennial away from their couch and Netflix than a friend reaching out with an invitation to join them.

Co-creation, as juxtaposed with relying on lay people alone to host gatherings, also provides the opportunity for professional staff to elevate participant-generated ideas by connecting them to high quality resources. For example, soon after launching The Well, the local Moishe House reached out asking if The Well would like to partner on a Christmas eve, Chinese Food + Shabbat Chanukah party. Their plan for the program was to light candles, eat Chinese food and Chanukah gelt, and then go out to the bars. By virtue of entering into a process of co-creation together with house residents and a couple of additional lay leaders, I was able to connect the group with JDC Entwine so they could provide us with materials to share about Jewish life in China, and I arranged for a resident of Moishe House Beijing to Skype into the gathering and answer questions about what it's like being a Jewish Millennial living in China. At the suggestion of one of the lay leaders, we created an accessible Chanukah blessings sheet, and provided plastic *Chanukiot*[161] and boxes of candles for those attending to take home with them. The co-creative process clearly elevated the quality and substance of the gathering.

---

[161] "Chanukiot" is the plural form of "Chanukiah" which is the special candelabra used during the holiday of Chanukah (often mistakenly/colloquially referred to as a "menorah").

#Friendseder

One of the best examples of co-creation leading to desired outcomes at The Well was the creation of #Friendseder.[162] At a leadership retreat with many of our most active co-creators taking place the weekend before Thanksgiving, we spent a few hours in breakout sessions brainstorming how we wanted to mark upcoming holidays. In the Passover breakout session, a comically large Post-it Note was stuck to the wall and was full of creative ideas. In passing, someone mentioned they were attending a Friendsgiving gathering the next evening, and a participant in the breakout said, "Wait. What if we did a Friendseder?"

A major national trend has taken off among Millennials who are getting together with their friends for "Friendsgiving"—a meal in the week or two leading up to the Thanksgiving holiday—so they can celebrate together before heading home to their families for the actual holiday.[163] The Well had for years embraced using secular models familiar to Millennials in order to help empower them Jewishly, so creating #Friendseder in order to empower them to host Passover Seder[164] gatherings with their friends was a no-brainer!

The Passover Seder is one of the most widely practiced Jewish rituals in the world, but often involves Millennials traveling home to be with their families, relying on older generations to curate those experiences. The majority of Jewish Millennials live in just a handful

---

[162] What's the deal with the hashtag (aka "the pound sign") in front of the word? The hashtag (#) is what allows one to feel they're participating in something bigger than themselves. Clicking on a hashtag in various social media platforms allows you to browse through posts of others who have used that hashtag. Our co-creators were excited to inspire global connections, envisioning hundreds of hosts around the world capturing images of their #Friendseder gatherings, and sharing them on social media so that the global Jewish community could feel connected in shared ritual.

[163] Ashley Fetters, "How Friendsgiving Took Over Millennial Culture." *The Atlantic*, Nov. 15, 2018.www.theatlantic.com/family/archive/2018/11/millennials-friendsgiving-history/575941.

[164] The Passover Seder is a ritual storytelling evening that recalls the liberation of the ancient Israelites from being slaves in Egypt. The word *Seder* itself means "order," as traditionally the evening's agenda is comprised of 15 specific steps performed in order.

of states[165] and many have cultivated "urban families." #Friendseder would allow us to empower Jewish Millennials to host a Passover Seder experience for themselves and their friends, and in the process share their own family rituals with friends, try out new ones, and hopefully enhance their own family Seders with what they learned (not to mention be better prepared to take over leadership responsibilities of those Seders one day)!

Once the brilliant suggestion left the person's mouth, it was a sprint to co-create and execute the group's vision, as the holiday was only a few short months away. Friendsgiving gatherings are traditionally held in the weeks leading up to the actual holiday, but our group decided #Friendseder gatherings could be held before, during or after the holiday. Shabbat dinner #Friendseder? Amazing! Wednesday evening #Friendseder and board game competition? Fantastic! Pizza party to end Passover #Friendseder? Game on! The goal was to frame the Passover Seder as both relevant and exciting, while consciously addressing the three core pain points of time, dollars, and confidence.

With support from the Charles and Lynn Schusterman Family Foundation's Grassroots Events initiative, we built a website full of resources (friendseder.com), including recipes, decor ideas, out-of-the-box Seder activities and more—some from The Well, and some from partner organizations such as OneTable, Hazon, InterfaithFamily (now known as 18Doors), Reboot, Moishe House, Keshet, and Haggadot.com. We also created our own professionally designed #Friendseder *Haggadah*[166] and made it available for download at no cost due to the generosity of donors, hosted "how-to-host" webinars, and had our full staff team at the ready for one-on-one coaching sessions with people from all over the country.

---

[165] "Nearly two-thirds [of millennials] live in just five states: NY, CA, FL, IL, and NJ."Leonard Saxe et al., "American Jewish Population Estimates 2020 Summary and Highlights." Brandeis University, 2021. www.brandeis.edu/cmjs/constructs/2016/millennials.html.

[166] A *Haggadah* is the ritual storytelling guidebook traditionally used at a Passover Seder.

Some asked, "Won't it be weird to do a Seder not on the Seder nights themselves?" Well, it's no weirder than the myriad Seders that happen before or during the holiday throughout the Jewish world—whether those are chocolate Seders, interfaith Seders, women's Seders, diplomatic Seders, and more. Our tradition encourages us to prepare spiritually for upcoming holidays. Whether it's blasting the shofar each day during the entire month of *Elul* leading up to the High Holidays or not eating meat for the nine days leading up to *Tisha B'Av*, we know that jumping into a holiday or observance often isn't as powerful as when we bring intention to getting in the mood![167]

In addition to dozens of #Friendseders being hosted in Metro Detroit that first Passover season, others were hosted all over the country, in Israel, and around the world. In the last few years, the concept has evolved and grown, and under The Well's new leadership is reaching more people than ever (they even created a #Friendseder board game!).

So, to break it down:

Time: We addressed time concerns by assembling materials such as recipes, a Haggadah, and a Seder shopping list on the website itself and by making it clear that #Friendseder gatherings could take place at the host's convenience and need not be held on a specifically designated night.

Dollars: We addressed cost concerns by providing modest subsidies for those hosting gatherings when needed, by partnering with Moishe House and OneTable to help provide hosting subsidies to those who fit into their eligibility criteria, making our custom *Haggadah* accessible at no cost due to the generosity of donors, and making it clear that potlucks, outings to restaurants where each pay their own way, and other choices were all acceptable options.

---

[167] Author Abigail Pogrebin goes into meaningful detail about her experience trying out these practices—including a Women's Seder—in her book *My Jewish Year* (Fig Tree Books, 2017).

Confidence: We addressed confidence with the how-to webinars and by making one-on-one coaching available to anyone in the world who wanted to host a #Friendseder.

Absent using the Empowerment-Centric Co-Creative model, our staff team would never have come up with this idea. By inviting our participants into the co-creative process from the earliest stages and working together to develop and execute the concept, there are Jewish Millennials around the world who have now experienced leading and/or attending a Passover Seder who otherwise might not have, and who felt empowered to make it their own.

Partnerships

The Empowerment-Centric Co-Creation model isn't limited to situations in which you're working with laity; it's also applicable when working with professional staff from partner organizations. By Year 2 of The Well's existence we had partnered with over 30 local organizations, both Jewish and secular. Partnership can be tricky in the Jewish organizational world—particularly when organizations understand partnership differently. It wasn't uncommon for organizations to reach out to us to "partner," by which they meant using our brand equity to encourage Millennials to attend their organization's pre-planned programs, often housed in their buildings. When asked how our participants could be involved in helping to co-create the gathering they were planning, we were often met with blank stares.

That said, the only reason The Well was able to grow as quickly as we did was courtesy of partnerships with other local Jewish organizations, particularly with Repair the World. In the early days of Repair the World's presence in Detroit, they had a cohort of 5-6 Millennial "fellows" who were tasked with engaging Metro Detroit's Jewish Millennials in community service opportunities. The Detroit city director was a friend and we were able to cultivate a mutually beneficial partnership: The Well would partner with Repair the

World regularly on community service projects, helping to get the word out and allowing them to further their mission of inspiring Metro Detroit's Jewish Millennials to engage in regular acts of service. In return, we regularly included Repair The World's fellows in our co-creative process and benefited from their ability to help us set up, greet attendees, and break down gatherings, as they provided extra "professional" hands we desperately needed to supplement the efforts of our tiny staff team and lay leaders who often couldn't help with setting up for large events during traditional work hours.

Partnering can be frustrating at times. For example, sometimes one organization's team does significantly more work than their partner's team on a program, which can make sharing equal billing frustrating (especially when it comes to reporting to funders). When different organizations have different approaches to marketing (such as The Well's commitment to never using the word "Free!"), it can be challenging to come up with shared promotional language. It's also important to invite partners to join in the co-creation process at the outset; if you approach partners to join you after you've got a fully fleshed out idea, they often don't feel as great a sense of ownership over the gathering and may not work as hard toward its success.

In general, partnering was without question a net benefit for The Well. It was a key component of our community-building philosophy and helped us expose those we were touching to communal organizations they may not have been familiar with, allowing us to embrace our role as a community concierge. Rather than leaning into territorialism, our community's organizations and those they serve would without question benefit from a broad embrace of co-creative partnerships.

Core Takeaways

1. Millennials crave the opportunity to play an active role in shaping experiences for themselves and others. Make it a point to invite them to co-create with you!
2. Be intentional during co-creation to address the core 3 pain points: time, dollars, and confidence.
3. Never assume content knowledge when it comes to Millennials and Jewish ritual—you risk embarrassing and/or alienating those you're seeking to attract.
4. It takes much more work and time to use the Empowerment-Centric Co-Creation model than to simply plan a program yourself—but if your goal is to engage, connect, and empower, such that your organization is relational rather than transactional (giving you a better chance at an extended relationship), it's a must.
5. Don't waste your time recruiting Jewish Millennials to events or membership. Rather, empower them to have a creative ownership stake, and then let them reach out to their networks! When people are excited about what they're doing, they'll reach out to their friends, who will inevitably support them by attending/donating/etc.
6. Consider partnering strategically with other organizations to help fill in gaps in your expertise or staffing, as well as to help broaden your reach.

Discussion Questions

- How does our organization plan its programmatic offerings? Do we tend to organize top-down, or in partnership with our target audience?
- What does our organizational staffing structure look like, and what is our capacity to lean into a co-creation model?
- How can our organization thoughtfully address Millennial concerns over time, dollars, and confidence?
- How does our organization go about fostering partnerships with other organizations? Do we have a set of guidelines or best practices we use when partnering? When in the program development process do we tend to reach out and why?
- If *Field of Dreams* isn't the ideal model going forward, what other movies can we look to for inspiration?

chapter 6

The High Cost of "Free"

Abraham paid out to Ephron the money that he had
named in the hearing of the Hittites—four hundred
shekels of silver at the going merchants' rate.
—Genesis 23:16

Immediately after his wife Sarah passes, Abraham seeks out a burial plot for her. When the locals express a willingness to gift him a plot, he refuses multiple times. Instead, he strikes a bargain with their leader that he will pay the fair market rate for a particular plot of land so that none could ever question his legitimate ownership of it.

We've come a long way since Abraham. If I had to take a guess as to which word one would be most likely to find on a promotional advertisement created by a Jewish organization striving to reach and attract Millennials, it wouldn't be "Jewish," or "Torah," or "God," or "Mitzvah." It wouldn't even be the name of the organization. It would be the word "Free!" The approach for decades now to try to entice Jewish Millennials to participate in Jewish life has been to charge them nothing. And unlike Abraham, many in the Jewish organizational world have embraced the language of "Free!"

To be fair, using "Free!" as a marketing technique is nothing new in the corporate world. Whether it's a free 8-week subscription to a newspaper, Red Bull hiring brand ambassadors to hand out free samples at college parties, or local karate studios inviting your child to try their first class for free, "Free!" can get people to interact with your business or product when they may not otherwise. Generally, people have "an irrational urge to jump for a FREE! item" even when it's not what they really want. Professor Dan Ariely writes in his book *Predictably Irrational* that this is likely because while "most transactions have both an upside and a downside, when something is FREE! we forget the downside."[168] So "Free!" is admittedly a highly effective marketing tool to get people in the door.

In 2013, Dr. David Bryfman, at the time the Chief Innovation Officer for the Jewish Education Project in New York, gave an ELI Talk (a Jewish TED Talk) called "The Value of Jewish Learning and Living in the 21st Century."[169] In it, he questions whether Jewish engagement should be free. While acknowledging that "Free!" can add value as a low barrier to access entry point, he simultaneously expresses concern that "Free!" has potential negative consequences we need to be aware of as a community and may not be in our best interests in the long term. After all, most of us will try something at least once if it's free. Who doesn't love the free samples at Costco? A decade later, our community has yet to truly grapple with his arguments, and has taken an even more extreme approach at times, going beyond "Free," to compete for the attention of Millennials (and now Gen-Z).

Author Daniel Pink, in his book *Drive*, seeks to understand intrinsic and extrinsic motivation—that is, what inspires people to do what we do. He spends significant time discussing the impact of incentives such as "Free!" Pink strikes a cautious tone, noting that sometimes, by introducing an incentive and then removing the incentive later, it makes the person less likely to participate in the desired activity than if the incentive had never been introduced in the first place.[170] It's entirely possible that by incentivizing Millennials to participate in Jewish life by marketing and offering programs

---

[168] Dan Ariely, *Predictably Irrational* (Harper Collins, 2008), 60.

[169] David Bryfman, "The Value of Jewish Learning and Living in the 21st Century." My Jewish Learning. www.myjewishlearning.com/eli-talks/the-value-of-jewish-learning-and-living-in-the-21st-century.

[170] Daniel H. Pink, *Drive* (Riverhead Books, 2011), 39.

as "Free!", we may be destroying any intrinsic motivation they may have had to participate in Jewish life.

Like Dr. Bryfman, and informed by Pink's work, I'm not convinced the Jewish community is approaching this issue with the intentionality we need to. We've effectively trained Millennials to view Jewish life as something they're entitled to if and when they want it without having to invest in it meaningfully. For a community that has built up tremendous infrastructure which relies on dues and charitable contributions to sustain it, a rising generation having been taught that Jewish life doesn't require any investment from them is a real problem. It's okay if we want programs for Millennials to be powered by philanthropy. But we'd better make sure we're training the next generation of philanthropists in the process!

Birthright

Birthright Israel is the first example that likely comes to people's minds when thinking about Jewish engagement and "Free!" Founded in 1999, since its inception Birthright Israel has brought over 800,000 unique participants (overwhelmingly Millennials) on a "Free 10 Day Trip to Israel!" It's well documented that the trip and organization were founded partially as a response to the 1990 National Jewish Population Study finding that more than 50% of non-Orthodox Jews were intermarrying,[171] with only 28% of those who were intermarrying raising their children Jewish.[172] The trip was conceived of as an educational intervention for young adults with the goals of ensuring Jewish continuity and a commitment to Israel. While never publicly acknowledged as a core goal of the trip, the desire for Jewish endogamy—Jews marrying other Jews—was

---

[171] Barry A. Kosmin et al., "Highlights of the CJF 1990 National Jewish Population Survey." The Council of Jewish Federations, 1991. www.jewishdatabank.org/content/upload/bjdb/ Highlights_of_the_CJF_1990_National_Jewish_Population_Survey_Summary_Report_ v3.pdf, 14.
[172] Kosmin, 16.

certainly one of the motivating factors behind its creation. One of Birthright's co-founders even paid for Caribbean honeymoons for couples who met on the trips and married.[173]

I have staffed several Birthright Israel trips and have experienced firsthand their transformative power for participants. I've also officiated at the weddings of several couples who met on those trips. As shared in the Introduction, my initial inspiration for launching The Well came while staffing a Birthright trip. Birthright has had a tremendous impact on the Jewish people! Long-term research data from Brandeis University's Cohen Center for Jewish Studies led by Professor Len Saxe has shown that participants on Birthright trips are much more likely to be active participants in the Jewish community in the long run than those who didn't go on the trip.[174]

Interestingly, there were significant debates between Birthright's co-founders as to whether the trip should be free.[175] While the data certainly indicate that those who went on a Birthright trip have much stronger Jewish communal ties than those who didn't, I can't help but wonder if the co-founders made a significant mistake by advertising the trip as "Free!", as they turned something that previously had required an investment into an entitlement. Clear victims of their choice to market a free 10-day trip were the organizations that had been running summertime Israel trips for high-school-aged teenagers. Such trips lasted for multiple weeks as opposed to only 10 days, allowing participants to form deeper connections with one another and the country, and for them to have a stronger connection to Israel heading into their college years (where potential hostility toward Zionists and Zionism often await on campus). However, many parents understandably questioned spending thousands of

---

[173] Michael Steinhardt, *Jewish Pride* (Wicked Son, 2022), 230.
[174] Graham Wright et al., "Birthright Israel's First Decade of Applicants: A Look at the Long-term Program Impact." Brandeis University, Nov. 2020. https://scholarworks.brandeis.edu/esploro/outputs/report/Jewish-Futures-Project-Birthright-Israels-First/9924144319601921, 1.
[175] Steinhardt, 142.

dollars for a trip for their high schooler when their child could take a "Free!" trip only a couple years later. For many years, having gone on a teen trip to Israel disqualified you from being eligible to go on a Birthright trip. Combined, these factors significantly reduced teen Israel trip enrollment numbers.[176]

I've always wondered what would have happened if, from the outset, Birthright had required some sort of modest financial contribution in order to participate in the trip. Something to have participants have some "skin in the game." Some would argue that participants were investing their time, but with the trips aligned with academic breaks, for those who were undergraduate or graduate students when they went on the trip I think it'd be a stretch to argue they were really giving up their time. Courtesy of not having invested anything personally in the trip, participants have been known to exhibit some poor behaviors.[177] Israel's Saturday Night Live equivalent, *Eretz Nehederet*, has parodied some of the less flattering behaviors exhibited on Birthright trips on their show.[178]

To reserve one's place on a Birthright Israel trip, participants are required to put down a $250 deposit. At the end of the trip, those dollars are refunded to the participants. I acknowledge it's easy to second guess the co-founders' decision, but what if Birthright had put a modest price tag on the trip, still allowing for it to be meaningfully subsidized, and then made robust financial aid available to ensure that regardless of means, their target audience could participate? Or what if from the outset, the $250 deposit from each participant had been pooled into a group fund, with the participants then having the chance to function as a giving circle[179] and to col-

---

[176] Joe Eskenazi, "Teen trips suffer from Birthright Israel's popularity." *J. The Jewish News of Northern California*, Apr. 4, 2008. www.jweekly.com/2008/04/04/teen-trips-suffer-from-birthright-israel-s-popularity.

[177] Nathan Guttman, "Is Birthright To Blame for Sexual Harassment on Trip?" *Forward*, Aug. 25, 2015. www.forward.com/news/319685/birthright.

[178] Prepare to laugh! https://vimeo.com/35660324

[179] For more on Jewish giving circles, visit: www.amplifiergiving.org/circles.

lectively donate to an Israeli charity of their choice, using part of the trip to educate about the role, importance and impact of Jewish philanthropy? Or what if that $250 had simply been contributed to the Birthright Foundation?

Some number of years into running trips, Birthright decided to give participants the option to donate their deposit dollars to the organization to "pay it forward." And yet, only a small percentage of those who have gone on the trips have done so.[180] With over 800,000 participants at $250 each, they'd have over $200,000,000 in their Foundation right now—and that doesn't even include any interest that would have accrued over the past 20+ years! With Birthright cutting back the number of trips they're running each year due to funding challenges,[181] I can't help but wonder if Birthright could have organizationally obtained similar positive outcomes using a more sustainable funding model—one more intentionally geared toward educating participants about the value and impact of Jewish philanthropy.

We'll Pay You!

Birthright by no means is alone when it comes to advertising things as "Free!"[182] Campus Hillels have historically been a meaningful Birthright Israel partner, often recruiting students and staffing buses with their Hillel staff. At campus Hillels, just about everything is marketed as "Free!" in order to attract students to participate. The assumption is that at their particular life stage, students are comparatively without disposable income. As a result, if you want to attract college students, you offer programs for "Free!" If there's food pro-

---

[180] "A Look at How Birthright Israel Trips Are Funded." Birthright Israel Foundation, May 1, 2020. www.birthrightisrael.foundation/blog/a-look-at-how-birthright-israel-trips-are-funded.
[181] Andrew Lapin, "Birthright Israel to scale back again, slashing number of free trips by up to a third." *Jewish Telegraphic Agency*, Nov. 21, 2022. www.jta.org/2022/11/21/israel/birthright-israel-to-scale-back-again-slashing-number-of-free-trips-by-up-to-a-third.
[182] For example, if you sign up for PJ Library, you can receive a free Jewish-themed book in the mail each month for your child(ren). www.pjlibrary.org.

vided that's better than what's on offer at the campus dining hall, it's a huge draw. Happy students filling seats in Hillel buildings certainly helps with fundraising efforts from their parents and grandparents (especially if you can capture photos and share them)! I've been a Senior Jewish Educator on campus—I get it. There is an inherent tension in many of our community's organizations between getting the largest number of *tushes* in seats possible in order to justify our work to funders while simultaneously striving to employ ecosystem strategies developed by leadership.

A Hillel program called the "Jewish Learning Fellowship" recently launched across the country courtesy of Hillel International's Office of Innovation. Modeled after similar programs that have been run for decades by Orthodox outreach rabbis on campuses around the world, the fellowship gathers a cohort for 10 weekly "experiential and conversational" learning sessions during the course of a college semester so that participants can deepen their understanding of Judaism. An admirable opportunity to be sure—especially since many of these college students haven't done any sort of "Jewish Learning" since their Bar/Bat/B-Mitzvah preparations, if at all.

It would be dreamy if students participating in such a fellowship prioritized setting aside a few dollars to invest in their Jewish growth. Recognizing the unlikeliness of that happening in a college setting, one could argue that having the programs offered at no cost to participants, with dinner provided, should be sufficient. However, the Jewish Learning Fellowship program has gone further, paying a stipend to students who participate. If you attend all 10 sessions and participate in a Shabbat experience, you get a check for hundreds of dollars. There are now some Hillels, such as the one at Michigan State University, offering as much as $350, because their original offer of $200 wasn't enough.[183] Why wasn't $200 enough you ask? Because the Chabad on campus was running their competing pro-

---

[183] https://www.msuhillel.org/jlf

gram, "Sinai Scholars," which offered a $350 stipend while only re-
quiring 8 sessions.[184] Jewish organizations on campus are literally
competing with one another over who can pay more (using donor
dollars) to attract the attention of Jewish students.

I understand the argument in favor of such a model.

It goes something like this:

> Without the financial incentive, many fewer students
> would participate in JLF due to competing opportu-
> nities for their attention, including the need for many
> to hold down part-time jobs in order to have spend-
> ing money. We're so confident that students will love
> what they find in the classes that we're willing to pay
> them to make Jewish Learning a priority in their
> otherwise busy lives, and the Jewish community will
> benefit by having a better educated population who'll
> make more Jewish choices and be more likely to sup-
> port Jewish causes and institutions in the long run
> as a result. So too, the 10-session commitment gives
> Hillel staff the chance to build relationships with the
> participants and to then leverage those relationships
> into more active participation and leadership roles at
> their campus Hillel. The incentive gets them in the
> door, but because it's an extended commitment and
> not a "one-off," it's worth it.

In addition, there are Talmudic-era rabbis who believed that
people engaging in Torah study—even if due to some sort of incentive—would lead to further engagement in Torah study absent
incentives down the road. "Rav Yehuda says that Rav says: A person

---

[184] https://www.jewishspartans.com/templates/articlecco_cdo/aid/5826968/jewish/Sinai-
Scholars.htm

should always engage in Torah study and performance of a mitzvah, even if he does not do so for their own sake, because by engaging in them not for their own sake, he will ultimately come to engage in them for their own sake."[185] Rabbi Yehuda teaches that his teacher Rav believed so strongly in the compelling nature of Torah study that even if it took an incentive to expose people who'd otherwise never self-select to engage in it, he was in favor. So there's an argument to be made that by virtue of offering these kinds of incentives, it signals how strongly we believe in its value.

What Is Jewish Life Worth?

On the other hand, I worry that by offering everything for free, or going beyond and paying young people to make Jewish choices, we're creating mercenaries rather than loyal soldiers and cheapening Jewish life and wisdom in the process. What is paying people to engage in Jewish study going to do to their innate motivation to engage in Jewish study and Jewish life in the future? Whatever happened to "you get what you pay for"?

After their college years, Millennials were met by Chabad, Moishe House, and other outreach organizations focused on 20-something-year-olds. Many of these organizations similarly use "Free!" as a marketing tactic, with some serving free alcohol as a draw.[186] Is it any wonder, after so much exposure to "Free!" (let alone being paid to do Jewish), Millennials aren't lining up to spend their disposable income on Jewish experiences or supporting Jewish organizations the way previous generations did?

People constantly take for granted the existence of our Jewish communal institutions. The core question becomes how we can shift Millennial mindsets; letting them know that as the beneficiaries of

---

[185] Babylonian Talmud, Sanhedrin, Folio 105b.

[186] Gary Rosenblatt, "Back Off On The Bacchanalia." *New York Jewish Week*, Mar. 30, 2011. www.jta.org/2011/03/30/ny/back-off-on-the-bacchanalia.

Jewish philanthropy for so many years that it's now time for them, as adults, to invest in Jewish life—especially if they want the community's institutions to be there when they feel they might need them. At the same time, we need to be conscious of potential sticker shock and to be prepared for how we'll deal with the folks who inevitably say, "Well, I'm not prepared to pay" and walk away.

Moving Past *Free*

We can achieve our communal education and engagement goals without using the word "Free!" as a marketing tool. We've relied on it too much, and our community's organizations are paying the price for it. There are two key ways we can move away from "Free!" First, we can commit to educate with intention toward philanthropy; second, we can use professionally designed experiences, then charge fair market prices for them.

While the word "Free" is sexy, it doesn't tell the whole story, because whatever the experience or product is, it obviously isn't free to produce! Hillel students may not be paying to attend "Free!" Shabbat dinners, but each of those meals has an associated cost, from the food, to its preparation, to the staffing, to the physical facility overhead and upkeep where the meal is being eaten, and more. Birthright Israel has a price tag north of $3,000 per participant. That obviously isn't "free."

When launching The Well, we made the conscious decision to never advertise anything as "Free!" For gatherings where we didn't feel the need to charge, our marketing materials included the language: "No cost to you due to the generosity of donors." For gatherings where we charged a subsidized amount, our advertisements said: "Subsidized cost thanks to the generosity of donors: $X." And when possible, we'd add in an additional line that said, "Actual cost: $Y." As an organization committed to education and helping to uplift many of the community's existing institutions, it was important to use our marketing materials as a mechanism to help the Millennial population we were serving understand what it actually costs to execute community gatherings, and to make sure they knew donors were investing in them, so that they too would be inspired to invest in Jewish community.

By no means is this the only way to educate toward philanthropy and community investment, and admittedly our phrasing took up more space and was clunkier than "Free!" However, we wanted to play a meaningful role in helping to transition Millennials from having a sense of entitlement to embracing a willingness to invest. Educating those we served about the real costs associated with executing a gathering was a valuable technique—particularly when catering to a generation that values transparency.

What to Expect

Speaking of transparency, one of the most effective techniques to market a gathering was including a "what to expect" section on the ad. As discussed earlier, Millennials are often wary of the intentions of institutions. An easy way to calm those nerves is to lay out what to expect at a particular gathering so that there's no confusion.

For example, here's the language we used in the Facebook Event invitation for our Swiss & Schvitz Shavuot celebration:

In partnership with Zach Berg of Mongers' Provisions, The Schvitz Health Club, and Detroit City Moishe House, we are excited to present
Swiss + Schvitz:
A Shavuot Experience for young adults ages 21-40.

The Jewish holiday of Shavuot celebrates the anniversary of receiving the Torah, and we'll be celebrating by enjoying copious amounts of dairy (a long-standing Jewish tradition). Spend some quality time

---

with fellow Metro Detroiters in a recently reclaimed historic Detroit bath house, while sampling various cheeses and immersing yourself in this major Jewish holiday!

Due to the generosity of donors, tickets are available for $25 (actual cost per person is $55), and include full access to The Schvitz (sauna, steam room, and cold pool), as well as cheese tasting with Zach Berg and Jewish learning about the holiday with Rabbi Dan! (Want to learn more about the Schvitz? Check out their website: https:// schvitzdetroit.com/)

WHAT TO EXPECT:
» Young adult crowd
» Doors open at 7:45pm; guided cheese tasting starts promptly at 8:00pm
» BYOB (Beer and wine only)
» Access to steam room, sauna, and cold pool
» Bring your own flip flops and robe; towels are provided
» This is an all-gender event, so swimwear is mandatory!

If saunas, steam rooms, and cold pools aren't your thing - no sweat! There will be board games, music, and nosh available after the cheese tasting and learning!

Special thanks to our awesome host committee:
Laura Feldman, Ian Gross, Angela Reich, Ethan Siegel,
Eric Shapiro, David Metler, and Kara Desmond!

Note the language choices. We acknowledge the tickets are subsidized and share the actual cost per person. We name our partner organizations as well as our host committee members, which makes them all feel great. We make clear who is invited (all genders welcome, ages 21-40). We share what to expect at the gathering, what you need to bring with you, and address concerns that might arise from folks who aren't interested in using The Shvitz's facilities. We also entice attendees to arrive on time (and not just waltz in anytime they feel like it during the evening) by making clear what time the guided cheese tasting—a core attraction of the gathering—is taking place. What does Shavuot have to do with Schvitzing? Absolutely nothing. Did it matter? Absolutely not. We sold every available ticket, and the entire crowd studied texts about why we consume dairy products on the holiday.

Lessons from JDate

One of the most remarkable game-changers for the Jewish community in the past 30 years has been the impact and success of JDate. Given the hysteria that emerged in response to the 1990 National Jewish Population Study, here was a solution, crafted for the digital/internet age, that not only helped address a core expressed concern for the Jewish community at the time—Jews finding other Jews to marry and make Jewish babies with—but that was also a for-profit business. JDate helped the organized Jewish community accomplish its endogamy goals and made an unbelievable amount of money in the process as a private business, not in any way relying on Jewish philanthropy to sustain itself. A game changer! Many of the weddings I've officiated have been couples who met on JDate (although admittedly more recently, more have been courtesy of JSwipe, which caters to Millennials and was bought by JDate's parent company in 2015 after a legal battle over JSwipe's choice of name which JDate argued was too similar, courtesy of the "J"[187]).

As a Jewish community, we rarely focus our attention on addressing communal goals using for-profit models. We rely on our nonprofit philanthropic construct because it's what we know and

---

[187] Hannah Vaitsblit, "JDate Acquires JSwipe." *Tablet*, Oct. 16, 2015. www.tabletmag.com/sections/news/articles/jdate-aquires-jswipe.

it's comfortable. But what would it look like for our organizations, even if structured as nonprofits, to experiment with revenue-generating offerings? As we tried to diversify our revenue streams at The Well, we turned our attention to designing experiences that would allow us to meet our organizational goals while charging a fair market price, with a strategy of embracing models from the secular world we knew Millennials were willing to pay for and making them Jewish.

Escaping From Egypt
(and the belief that Millennials won't pay!)

So, imagine the following:

It's the Saturday evening before Passover. You find yourself and a group of friends entering an airy, well-lit loft in a hip neighborhood. Your mission: to find the items needed to populate the Seder plate sitting empty on the large Passover Seder table set in the middle of the room. You take a sip of horseradish infused vodka before the clock starts, which puts you in the mood not only for Passover, but for a challenge. That's when you hear it: Click. The sound of being locked into the room with only 45 minutes to escape.

Hundreds of young adults in Metro Detroit experienced this moment of excitement in the week leading up to Passover in 2018, ready to take on The Well's "Escape From Egypt"—a professionally designed Passover Seder-inspired escape room. Too often in the Jewish community, we mimic existing models but don't execute them in a professional way, resulting in a subpar experience for participants who are then reluctant to participate in future communal offerings. After researching and not finding anyone selling the rights to a professionally designed Passover escape room, we commissioned a professional escape room designer in Los Angeles to create a custom experience. We didn't try to design our own or look for instructions on Google. We hired a professional and relied on his expertise to craft the puzzles while we infused substantive Jewish content. We sublet a loft apartment in the cool part of town and transformed it into the escape room and ran it commercially for a week leading up to Passover to help folks get excited about, learn about, and connect with the holiday.

Our market research indicated that the average local escape room charged $18-$25 per person to participate. We confidently charged $100 per group, for a group of up to 8 people (a lump-sum price encouraged folks to bring friends to help share the costs, helping us reach that many more people). We made sure that whether one was a biblical scholar or had never heard the word "Passover" before, there was equal opportunity (and challenge) in solving the puzzles. And because we were offering a professional product and using quality marketing materials designed by a professional graphic designer, we received excellent media buzz and excited feedback from our Millennial participants (who overwhelmingly said they learned something new about the Passover holiday), and who then referred others our way. Word got out such that we even had church groups participate! In the end, we not only accomplished our educational and engagement goals for Passover, but we welcomed hundreds of participants and earned thousands of dollars in ticket sales.

Admittedly, the dollars we earned only covered the cost of commissioning the game itself. We were also worried that the novelty of the game would no longer be particularly exciting in Metro Detroit the following year. So we put together a "How To" guide, complete with links to supplies needed, explanations of the various puzzles, diagrams to direct room set-up and more. We then asked one of our active participants, who happens to be a patent attorney, to draw up documents for us so that we could license the game out to other organizations around the country. We offered licensing rights for $500 and told organizations to expect supplies to also cost about $500. So, for only $1,000 organizations could run our Passover Escape

Room (which we had spent more than \$5,000 to create) in their communities. We also made one of our staff members available at all hours to field questions that might arise in the weeks leading up to Passover to help troubleshoot any issues.

It was quite exciting to see our Passover Escape Room pop up in several other cities the next year! However, when reaching out to potential licensees, such as campus Hillels, JCCs, and synagogues, the two most common responses we received were: "I'm sorry but we don't have \$1,000 to spend on a Passover program," and/or "I'm sorry but we simply don't have the staff bandwidth to execute this." This was a learning moment for us, as even though we were reaching out to organizations with significantly larger budgets and staff teams than our own and providing them with an affordable and proven money-making opportunity that could simultaneously help them achieve Jewish educational objectives while appealing to a desired demographic group, there were only a handful who felt they had the capacity to capitalize on the opportunity.

It's All About Demonstrating Value

As a Jewish community, when we're offering something at a subsidized price (or for "free") as a means of drawing in customers or participants, we won't get repeat business or patronage from Millennials absent demonstrating the value of our offerings. Incentivizing people to participate in Jewish life does not inherently lead to an investment in the community. Millennials are ready and willing to pay for the things they value and what they've been socialized to want. Pelotons, avocado toast, escape rooms and iPhones are expensive, and Millennials have no problem paying for them. But what Millennials do have a problem paying for is experiences that are subpar courtesy of not being professionally designed and executed, or services they aren't using. As Rabbi Hayim Herring writes in his book *Tomorrow's Synagogue Today*, "the majority… will only pay for services they use personally and will not support a congregation simply because it is a good cause."[188]

So what would it look like to create models where people can pay only for the services they're using? In the corporate world, we find "unbundling" being embraced as a core business tactic. What is unbundling? The Cambridge Dictionary defines it as "to start to sell a product or service separately when previously it had been sold together with others."[189] You're likely most familiar with this tactic when it comes to how television has changed in recent years courtesy of streaming services. Why pay hundreds of dollars a month for cable television which allows you to have all the channels (most of which you never watch) when you can pay $8.99 a month for Hulu or $10.99 a month for Disney+ to get only the channels you want to watch and save lots of money in the process? As discussed earlier, customization is now the American cultural expectation, and in many ways it is a reflection of personal identity.[190]

As a community, we need to rethink how we "bundle" our services; in particular, we really have no choice but to embrace "unbundling" when it comes to organizational membership dues by creating different packages that meet the needs and desires of our target audiences, even going so far as to allow them to customize their selections. Rabbis Kerry and Avi Olitzky, in their book *New Membership & Financial Alternatives for the American Synagogue*, refer to this as "special-interest membership."[191] To use synagogues as an example: if your average Millennial is attending synagogue services exclusively on Rosh Hashanah and Yom Kippur and isn't using any other synagogue offering with regularity, they aren't going

---

[188] Hayim Herring, *Tomorrow's Synagogue Today* (Rowman & Littlefield, 2012), 38.

[189] https://dictionary.cambridge.org/us/dictionary/english/unbundle.

[190] Julie Beck, "Fancy Starbucks Drinks and the Special Snowflakes Who Order Them." *The Atlantic*, May 13, 2016. www.theatlantic.com/health/archive/2016/05/food-customization-america/482073

[191] Kerry M. Olitzky & Avi S. Olitzky, *New Membership and Financial Alternatives for the American Synagogue* (Jewish Lights, 2015), 95.

to pay a blanket membership rate of $2,000 a year. But they might be willing to pay for a stand-alone ticket to High Holiday services (many synagogues already offer High Holiday tickets independent of membership for a designated price). Families with children who want to enroll in religious school would have a different package tailored to their specific needs and life stage as well. You get the idea.

Some have frustratedly referred to this concept as "a la carte" Judaism. Their expressed concern is that if we just let people pick and choose the parts of Jewish life they want to participate in and support financially, not only will it threaten the business models of our legacy organizations, but it will destroy the entire Jewish ecosystem, not to mention eliminate any real chance of cultivating deep, loving, intergenerational community. I hear and understand this concern.

Via unbundling, the opportunity exists to reach a broader customer base. While each individual purchaser might end up spending less than the institution's "full dues" amount, by putting together attractive packages, the potential exists to reach more people. The average dollar amount invested may be less per family unit, but the opportunity exists to attract many more family units when they get to choose the services they want, offsetting any associated losses. When designing packages, our organizations can make "full dues" equivalents more attractive—just like the cable companies do—by making individual items pricier and offering discounts when multiple items are selected.

We can't expect people to pay for things they aren't actively using. As Rabbi Terry Bookman writes in *Beyond Survival*, "any institutional structure that automatically assumes Jewish loyalty is destined for the dust heap of history."[192] So it's incumbent upon those of us who value legacy Jewish organizations and the services they provide to demonstrate their value to Millennials as well as to the many other folks who aren't engaged in or affiliated with the organized Jewish community.

---

[192] Terry Bookman, *Beyond Survival* (Rowman & Littlefield, 2019), 101.

In the corporate world, this is called "value selling." Sales training authority and author Brian Tracy emphasizes that the key is to "teach people how much they will benefit, how much your product or service will help them, and all of the things your product or service can do to help them achieve their goals and solve their problems. The more you focus on these values, the less important price becomes."[193] While I know it's hard to think of our community's organizations as businesses, that's how they're structured. They do incredible work and provide meaningful services of all sorts, much of which is worth paying for and supporting. It's on us though to communicate the value proposition. We can't assume that our target population will value what we're offering.

When embracing an unbundling approach, while the construct may feel more transactional, the goal is still to form deep and meaningful personal relationships. We must provide a high quality and transformational experience for those who are using organizational offerings, build relationships with them, and help them make friends with other users. As Dr. Ron Wolfson writes in his book *Creating Sacred Communities*, "Your challenge is how to craft a community of people who are so engaged with each other and with the leaders of the community that they wouldn't think of quitting..."[194] Fostering friendships among users will undoubtedly strengthen their commitment to our organizations.

Making The Jewish Choice

Anecdotally, my experience is that many Jewish Millennials will make Jewish choices, all else being equal. For example, if there are two nursery schools a couple is considering sending their child to, one Jewish and one not, they'll pick the Jewish one provided that the quality, cost, hours, and distance are equal. But as soon as the Jew-

---

[193] Brian Tracy, "Value Selling: How To Sell Value Rather Than Price." Brian Tracy International. www.briantracy.com/blog/sales-success/how-to-sell-value-rather-than-price.
[194] Ron Wolfson and Brett Kopin, *Creating Sacred Communities* (The Kripke Institute, 2022), 10.

ish one is significantly more expensive, has less convenient hours, is closed for too many Jewish holidays when the parents need to work (this is a real challenge), or is in a less convenient location, the average couple is much more likely to pick the non-Jewish option.

The same holds true when it comes to executing Jewish experiences for Millennials. Millennials are willing to pay fair market value for Jewish experiences provided the experiences are of the same professional caliber they would have in a secular setting. All else being equal, they'll pick the Passover escape room option over the other secular escape room option. But if they're met with an inferior product or experience, one that feels ad-hoc and cheap as opposed to professionally executed, they won't make the Jewish choice. Unfortunately, too often in our community we haven't committed the resources to execute experiences that are on par with those you'd find in the secular private sector. In a world with nearly limitless experiences competing for one's time and attention, less-than-professional isn't going to cut it.

Not every organization is going to have the desire or resources to commission and create these kinds of experiences, and that's okay! Individual Jewish organizations and communities need not recreate the wheel—it's much cheaper to license content that has been created and piloted in other Jewish communities than to have everyone constantly creating from scratch. I'm surprised there hasn't been a more intentionally designed centralized clearinghouse across various national Jewish umbrella organizations to help distribute the best things that are working across the country into their constituent communities, especially given that we're in an era where local organizations are often questioning whether it makes sense to still affiliate with national umbrella organizations due to constantly asking, "What are we getting out of this relationship?"[195] There's a

---

[195] Stewart Ain, "As USCJ's Money Woes Ease, The Next Test Is To Win Over Critics." *New York Jewish Week*, Oct. 3, 2019. www.jta.org/2019/10/03/ny/as-uscjs-money-woes-ease-next-test-

need for a vehicle beyond email listservs and Dropboxes. As I had the privilege of brainstorming with Dan Libenson and Lex Rofeberg on an episode of the *Judaism Unbound* podcast,[196] what would it look like if there were a professionally designed and curated Jewish Etsy[197] equivalent where folks around the country could find high-quality, vetted, Jewish experiential education offerings they could purchase (or license) and execute in their communities? There is a clear need for meaningful, large-scale investment to create these kinds of offerings which are professionally designed, can be run all over the country with minimal expertise, and that Millennials (and others!) are willing to pay fair market value for, allowing our community's organizations to make money while accomplishing their Jewish education and engagement missions. Going forward, I hope our community's donors, who generously support so many "Free!" offerings, consider hedging their bets by simultaneously investing in models that require people to pay!

Core Takeaways

1. Consider eliminating the word "Free!" from your marketing/advertisements and proceed with caution when incentivizing Jewish experiences.
2. Educate toward philanthropy. Subsidize costs if and when appropriate, but make it clear what your services or gathering actually cost per person; emphasize that the reduced costs are due to the generosity of donors.

---

win-over-critics.

[196] Dan Libenson and Lex Rofeberg, "Escape from Egypt." *Judaism Unbound*, Episode 210, Feb. 21, 2020. www.judaismunbound.com/podcast/episode-210-dan-horwitz-passover.

[197] Etsy is a global online marketplace where people come together to make, sell, buy and collect unique items.

3. Bring great intention to demonstrating value and be ready to allow for your target consumers/participants/congregants to customize their selections to meet their needs.

4. Experiment with infusing Jewish content into secular commercial models Millennials are willing to pay fair market value for, execute them at a professional level, and make money!

5. Don't feel the need to recreate the wheel—find out who's building such models already and establish partnerships or licensing arrangements to bring them to your community!

Discussion Questions

• Does our organization currently use the word "Free" in our marketing materials? If so, should we continue to do so? Why or why not?

• In what ways does our organization educate toward philanthropy? How could we enhance and increase those?

• How do we let folks know what to expect at our organization's gatherings?

• What are our organization's core goals? What are for-profit models that might allow us to achieve them?

• What would it look like to "unbundle" our organization's services?

• How does our organization communicate our value proposition?

chapter 7

How to Raise $100K
from Millennials in Three Days

*Rav Asi says: Charity is equivalent to all
the other mitzvot combined.*
—*Babylonian Talmud, Bava Batra, Folio 9a.*

"Rabbi Dan, I'd like to make a $25,000 investment in The Well this year. Now, how can we best leverage those dollars in order to raise additional ones for the organization?"

These words, spoken by a young man in his early 30s over lunch, almost made me do a spit-take with my soup! Talk about a dream come true! Thankfully, I was able to swallow before expectorating,[198] collect my thoughts, and begin to brainstorm how best to leverage such an investment to grow participant financial commitments. What would you have said?

While you think on it, here's some key background info on American Jewish philanthropy:

The American Jewish philanthropic landscape is rapidly changing, with a reduction in small dollar donors accelerating the rise and power of mega-philanthropists, donor-advised funds and well-endowed family foundations.[199] Many Jewish Federations—the centralized umbrella philanthropic giving entity of the Jewish community (think the Jewish United Way) with branches in well over 100 North American cities—rely on 30-40% of the gifts they received

---

[198] Thank you to Gaston from *Beauty and the Beast* for teaching me this word.
[199] For a history of Jewish philanthropy, I recommend Lila Corwin Berman's book, *The American Jewish Philanthropic Complex* (Princeton University Press, 2020).

during the Yom Kippur War in 1973. That means that in the past 50 years there has been a roughly 60% decrease in the number of donors to the Federation system. The same is true of many national Jewish nonprofit organizations and "friends of" Israeli institutions: Fewer individuals are giving, but those who are giving tend to give large amounts, helping to offset the shortcomings.[200] What has commonly become embraced as the 80/20 rule in Jewish philanthropy (80% of the dollars comes from 20% of the donors)[201] in many communities has now shifted to the 90/10 rule (90% of the dollars coming from 10% of the donors).[202]

As organizations shift to relying more on big givers, fewer big givers are finding Legacy Organizations attractive. The institutions are caught in a comparative catch-22: they are often perceived as stagnant, so donors don't invest the funds needed to help them take innovative risks.[203] On the flip side, if organizations invest too heavily in innovation, they risk failing to deliver on their missions. And yet, despite the increased reliance on large donors, when asked by the Pew Research Center in 2020 "whether they made a financial donation to any Jewish charity or cause (such as a synagogue, Jewish school or group supporting Israel) in the 12 months prior to taking the survey," almost half of American Jewish respondents (48%) say they did."[204]

Contrary to popular belief, Millennials are willing to invest in the causes and organizations that speak to them. Even though Millennials earn 20% less than Baby Boomers did at the same stage of

---

[200] Jack Wertheimer, "Giving Jewish." The AVI CHAI Foundation, 2018. www.avichai.org/wp-content/uploads/2018/03/Giving-Jewish-Jack-Wertheimer.pdf, 9.
[201] In broader culture this is known as "The Pareto Principle"—named after economist Vilfredo Pareto—which posits that 80% of outcomes or outputs result from 20% of all causes or inputs.
[202] Wertheimer, 9.
[203] Wertheimer, 12.
[204] "Jewish Community and Connectedness." Pew Research Center, May 11, 2021. www.pewresearch.org/religion/2021/05/11/jewish-community-and-connectedness.

life (despite having higher levels of education),[205] almost 75% of Millennials made a charitable donation during the first six months of the Covid-19 pandemic—a higher percentage than any other generation.[206] A whopping 84% of Millennials give to charity annually. Granted, the average amount they donate annually is under $500.[207] While that might lead folks to question whether it makes sense to engage Millennials philanthropically, the answer is a resounding "yes, it's necessary!" given that the Baby Boomer generation is expected to pass down over $30 trillion to Millennials in the coming decades, who will then have the resources to donate more significant amounts.[208]

Philanthropy and Synagogues

It may seem odd to think about synagogue membership models and philanthropy in the same chapter, but the two are unquestionably intertwined. Like philanthropic giving to Jewish organizations, synagogue membership is on the decline outside of the Orthodox world, mimicking trends across religions.[209] Nationally, we've seen Reform and Conservative movement synagogue membership numbers decline.[210] In Metro Detroit, where synagogue affiliation rates have

---

[205] Reid Cramer et al., "The Emerging Millennial Wealth Gap." New America, Oct. 29, 2019. www.newamerica.org/millennials/reports/emerging-millennial-wealth-gap.

[206] Megan Leonhardt, "Nearly 3 out of 4 millennials have donated money during the pandemic." *CNBC*, Sep. 30, 2020. www.cnbc.com/2020/09/29/more-millennials-donated-money-during-the-pandemic-than-other-generations.html.

[207] "The Ultimate List Of Charitable Giving Statistics For 2023." Nonprofits Source, 2023. www.nonprofitssource.com/online-giving-statistics.

[208] Jack Kelly, "Millennials Will Become Richest Generation In American History As Baby Boomers Transfer Over Their Wealth." *Forbes*, Oct. 26, 2019. https://www.forbes.com/sites/jackkelly/2019/10/26/millennials-will-become-richest-generation-in-american-history-as-baby-boomers-transfer-over-their-wealth.

[209] Jeffrey M. Jones, "U.S. Church Membership Falls Below Majority for First Time." Gallup, Mar. 29, 2021. news.gallup.com/poll/341963/church-membership-falls-below-majority-first-time.aspx.

[210] "U.S. Jews Share Shuls Due to Low Attendance." *Haaretz*, Nov. 5, 2013. www.haaretz.com/jewish/2013-11-05/ty-article/.premium/u-s-jews-share-shuls-due-to-low-attendance/0000017f-e95f-df5f-a17f-fbdf8b410000.

tended to be higher than the national average historically,[211] there has been a significant drop over the past 15+ years. From 2005-2018, while Orthodox synagogue membership increased 16 percent to 1,900 households, membership in Conservative synagogues decreased 19 percent from 4,400 households to 3,500 households, and membership in local Reform congregations declined 13 percent from 7,250 households to 6,300 households.[212] Many synagogues are now dealing with fewer membership dollars coming in and are increasingly relying on philanthropy to make up the difference between the income and expense lines on their budgets.

The Jewish community's traditional synagogue business model generally resembles that of a fitness center, with membership dues giving you access to the facility and certain services. But unlike synagogues, fitness centers can target market to every adult living within a certain distance of their facility regardless of religion, and fitness centers build their facilities to accommodate only 5-10% of their membership at any given time. For example, the average Planet Fitness has 6,500 members and can accommodate only 300 of them at any given time.[213] Synagogues, on the other hand, often have gigantic footprints. Many of today's large synagogue facilities were constructed in the 1950s, 60s and 70s due to a desire to show off Jews having "made it" in America and paralleling the construction of the interstate highway system and accompanying embrace of suburban living. Rabbi Daniel Judson observes in his book *Pennies for Heaven* that "Many synagogues were built for the High Holidays and not

---

[211] Ira Sheskin et al., "2018 Detroit Jewish Population Study." Jewish Federation of Metropolitan Detroit, Sep. 2018. www.jewishdatabank.org/content/upload/bjdb/Detroit_2018_Summary_Report_Jewish_Population_Study.pdf, 104.

[212] Shari Cohen, "The Future of Shul: Detroit Jewish Population Study Indicated Declining Synagogue Membership." *The Detroit Jewish News*, Aug. 6, 2020. www.thejewishnews.com/2020/08/06/the-future-of-shul-detroit-jewish-population-study-indicated-declining-synagogue-membership.

[213] Stacey Vanek Smith, "Why We Sign Up For Gym Memberships But Never Go To The Gym." *NPR*, Dec. 30, 2014. www.npr.org/sections/money/2014/12/30/373996649/why-we-sign-up-for-gym-memberships-but-don-t-go-to-the-gym.

for regular Sabbath usage."[214] The result is that far too many synagogues have physical footprints (and carrying costs for HVAC and
the like) beyond what the synagogue can afford, and well beyond
what they require 363 days a year. This has not only a concerning
financial impact, but also negative spiritual implications. As Rabbis
Joshua Stanton and Benjamin Spratt write in their book *Awakenings*,
"Given their high operating costs in money, time, and energy, our
sacred edifices become a purpose unto themselves, rather than the
manifestation of more important missions."[215]

To keep their doors open, synagogues have required philanthropic
investments, most often taking the form of general charitable giving,
tributes, Yom Kippur appeals, naming opportunities, and interest
earned on endowment investments. Simply put, philanthropy has
been and continues to be key to the survival of synagogues. Thankfully, according to American tax law, charitable contributions to
synagogues are tax deductible![216]

As documented by father/son duo Rabbis Kerry and Avi Olitzky
in their book *New Membership & Financial Alternatives for the American Synagogue*, there are new models beyond traditional membership now being used by many synagogues.[217] For example, many
communities are shifting to a purely philanthropic model, frequently
referred to as the "gift from the heart" model as a means of refram-
ing what it means to be part of a sacred community.[218] This model
suggests mimicking what the ancient Israelites did when it was time,
after the Exodus from Egypt, to bring offerings so that the Taberna-

---

[214] Daniel Judson, *Pennies for Heaven* (Brandeis University Press, 2019), 195.
[215] Joshua Stanton and Benjamin Spratt, *Awakenings* (Behrman House, 2022), 12.
[216] "Publication 526, Charitable Contributions." Internal Revenue Service, 2022.www.irs.gov/publications/p526#en_US_2021_publink1000229641.
[217] Some of those models are old ones that are becoming new again. After all, as we learn in Ecclesiastes (1:9): "There is nothing new under the sun."
[218] Kerry M. Olitzky & Avi S. Olitzky, *New Membership & Financial Alternatives for the American Synagogue* (Jewish Lights, 2015), 37.

cle[219] and its associated objects could be built.[220] No membership dues—rather, freewill gifts from those whose hearts moved them. The dream of course is to run into the problem that Moses then encountered, which was his artisans complaining that the people were bringing too much.[221] In response, Moses instructs the Israelites to stop bringing offerings—probably the first and only time in history where a Jewish organizational leader has said, "We have enough! Please stop with all the donations!"

Making a personally meaningful investment in an organization—one that comes from the heart—is much more likely to succeed with Millennials than the traditional membership model. A number of synagogues that have made this shift have been pleased to find some younger members joining (albeit with most paying an amount significantly less than the prior membership dues rate).[222] While the gift from the heart model may speak to some Millennials, as I shared in the last chapter I still think the "unbundling" approach is more likely to be successful in reaching the broadest possible audience. For a membership-phobic generation, there's value in eliminating membership from the conversation, and instead charging a fair market price for a synagogue's offerings with an eye toward building relationships in the process. Our experience at The Well helped clarify that while membership dues may be a turn off, Millennials are ready and willing to invest in and support the organizations they care about.

---

[219] The portable sanctuary that accompanied the Israelites during their wanderings in the desert.
[220] Exodus 35:29
[221] Exodus 36:5
[222] Michael Paulson, "The 'Pay What You Want' Experiment at Synagogues." *The New York Times*, Feb. 2, 2015. www.nytimes.com/2015/02/02/us/the-pay-what-you-want-experiment-at-synagogues.html.

Millennial Motivations

Millennials tend to draw a mental distinction between two types of organizations when it comes to thinking about investing/joining/donating.

I'll call the first category of organizations "charities." These are organizations where there is no expectation that you as the donor will benefit in a direct way from your donation. In the Jewish world, this grouping generally includes social service agencies who are helping those in need (and Jewish Federations—although umbrella giving is definitely its own animal within this category, as Millennials often want to see the direct impact of their investment which is challenging at times in the Federation model courtesy of its allocations construct and perceived lack of transparency). When Millennials give to these organizations, it's generally because they're inspired by the mission and see the impact of their donations. In fact, some even refer to Millennials as "Generation Impact" because they're so keen on seeing progress made on the issues they care about.[223] But it's also often because they are invited to do so by their friends. In the age of social media many donations are made via a single click on Facebook in response to friends sharing causes they're passionate about or when invited by friends to support them in their upcoming "race for the cure" type of events. Peer invitations (and peer pressure) absolutely influence Millennial giving practices![224]

The second category of organizations I'll call "investments." Technically not-for-profits or tax-exempt via "church" designation by the IRS, these organizations are ones that the investor is personally benefiting from. In the Jewish world, this grouping generally includes

---

[223] Erin Nylen-Wisocki, Review of *Generation Impact: How Next Gen Donors Are Revolutionizing Giving*, by Sharna Goldseker and Michael Moody. *Philanthropy News Digest*, Nov. 28, 2017. www.philanthropynewsdigest.org/features/book-reviews/generation-impact-how-next-gen-donors-are-revolutionizing-giving.

[224] "Millennial Giving & Volunteering Influenced By Peers." *The NonProfit Times*, June 24, 2015. www.thenonprofittimes.com/npt_articles/millennial-giving-volunteering-influenced-by-peers.

synagogues, JCCs, summer camps, Jewish schools, and the like. Unlike social service agencies, these organizations are generally run like businesses and often have "fee for service" financial models. For a Millennial to invest, they generally need to feel they have personally benefitted from the organization's work; they then invest so that they can continue receiving the benefit and/or so that others can receive the benefit they did and appreciate having received.

An interesting trend to note is that many Jewish Federations, to engage potential donors, regularly plan and host forward-facing programs in their communities. This allows them to position themselves with Millennial donors as both an investment and a charity, yielding a greater likelihood of contributions to their annual campaigns. However, these efforts in some ways step on the toes of their beneficiary agencies, such as JCCs whose traditional mandate is to offer communal programs. It's awkward to be perceived as competing with the organizations you're charged with financially supporting! This has led to the emergence in some smaller communities of integrated models where the JCC is part of the Federation as opposed to being structured as a separate organization. I wouldn't be surprised to see that trend grow in the future and make its way to larger cities as well.

Regardless of which category an organization falls into, an additional key component for Millennials is transparency.[225] Soon after ordination I had the privilege of serving as the organizational rabbi for Moishe House, the global leader in young adult Jewish engagement for those in their 20s. One of the highlights of my time at Moishe House was a national leadership development conference that brought together over 100 residents from the various North

---

[225] Shelley Hoss, "The Future Of Giving: Trends Shaping Next-Gen Philanthropy." *Forbes*, Dec. 27, 2021. www.forbes.com/sites/forbesnonprofitcouncil/2021/12/27/the-future-of-giving-trends-shaping-next-gen-philanthropy.

American houses for a long weekend together at a summer camp in Texas. One of the core sessions offered at the conference provided the opportunity for those in attendance—all Millennials—to attend a session with the organization's Founder and CEO David Cygielman (a Millennial himself), where he walked them through the organization's budget line by line. It was the most radical act of transparency I had ever seen from a nonprofit leader. This wasn't a boardroom. This wasn't a select panel of residents. This wasn't a presentation to potential large-scale funders. This was a session for the 20-something-year-olds in attendance who were interested in learning more about the organization's top and bottom lines with the opportunity to ask any and all questions. This is the kind of transparency I'm talking about when I say that Millennials want transparency from the organizations they support. As a result of that session, an incredibly large percentage of the participants in that room donated to Moishe House. Moishe House has subsequently built one of the most robust young adult donation campaigns in the country, with more than 2,200 residents, participants and alumni donating over $150,000 in 2022. For many organizations, it's going to be incredibly uncomfortable to embrace radical transparency and will prove to be a real culture shift. But the respect it garnered in that room was unbelievable and indicative of generational shifts we need to be aware of.

The Well's Approach to Fundraising

The Well, I'm sure it comes as no surprise, fell into the second "investment" category. We weren't a social service agency—we were some hybrid of a synagogue, JCC without walls, and/or grown-up Hillel,[226] and our fundraising philosophy was inspired by Chabad's approach, which has two core steps:

---

[226] The *2018 Slingshot Guide* referred to The Well as "the hipster cousin to the Jewish Community Center in your town." It's by far my favorite description of the organization to date.

1. Deliver a quality/transformational experience up front, such that people come to feel they're benefiting from the organization's work personally and feel connected to it.
2. Invite them to invest in the organization so that they—and others—can continue to enjoy the same sense of meaning, connection, and community.

As opposed to most fee-for-service organizations that ask for the investment (or "payment") up front, Chabad's approach is flipped. One of the foundational questions we asked when we started The Well was, "What would Chabad look like if it were liberal?" Being inspired by and embracing their fundraising approach felt natural.

Chabad emissaries, when they're sent all over the world, often receive three years of seed funding that gives them a runway to establish themselves, deliver quality experiences, and begin building authentic relationships without having to immediately solicit funds.[227] Thanks to generous seed funding from our pilot donor, The Well did not actively solicit investments from our participants until our third year of work. In anticipation of our seed funding being scaled back, we needed to build a philanthropic income line funded by our participants. After researching best practices and overlaying them onto our target audience, we chose to pilot a three-day relationship-based crowdfunding campaign, laying the groundwork for and working out the kinks in a strategy that would ultimately catapult our fundraising efforts in subsequent years.

We chose three days as the duration for the campaign; we wanted to create a sense of urgency and not let people say, "Okay, thanks for letting me know. I'll get to it eventually." Given that we needed to

---

[227] Rena Greenberg, "Chabad Families, Communities, Grow in Small, Remote Communities." *Chabad Lubavitch Headquarters*, Feb. 12, 2015. www.lubavitch.com/chabad-families-communities-grow-in-small-remote-communities.

compete in the attention economy,[228] our goal was for the person to be engaged and inspired to immediately take action and invest while we had their attention, reducing the amount of time and bandwidth we needed to spend on follow-up interactions. It's common for crowdfunding platforms like Kickstarter to advise users to use short campaigns to create a sense of urgency.[229]

We chose to focus our efforts in our first campaign on securing the largest number of donations possible rather than worrying about how much money we were raising. Our pitch was essentially "please invest something meaningful to you—and whether that's $5 or $500, all investments are so appreciated." We wanted to be able to demonstrate to our funders—present and future—that we had broad buy-in from the Millennials we were serving; and while they weren't in a place to fund the entirety of the organization themselves due to life-stage and modest incomes, they were still committed to investing in us. Practically speaking, this gave us an expansive list of donors to pull from and to encourage to give again (and at higher levels) the following year. It was the beginning of our donor database, and we wanted as broad a list as possible!

In that first fundraising campaign, we raised roughly $38,000 via more than 400 investments from Millennials we were serving (with one Millennial donor contributing $15,000, one donating $1,000, and everyone else donating at a more modest level). We were thrilled and had a solid platform to build on the next year.

---

[228] A concept developed by Nobel Laureate Herbert Alexander Simon, an American economist, political scientist and cognitive psychologist, which essentially posits that since human attention spans are limited, they are effectively a finite resource in the marketplace, and companies are in essence competing with one another for our limited attention.

[229] "What is the maximum project duration?" Kickstarter. Updated Feb. 2023. https://help. kickstarter.com/hc/en-us/articles/115005128434-What-is-the-maximum-project-duration.

Leveraging a Large Investment

Heading into Year 4, The Well had grown from an initial annual budget of $175,000 to an annual budget exceeding $400,000, supporting over 300 gatherings each year, 35 small groups meeting each month, hundreds of one-on-one coffee dates, constantly renting out Third Places, and a full-time staff team of four. The organization had been featured in the Slingshot Guide the previous two years, had been selected as one of the inaugural Open Dor Project spiritual startup communities, and had cultivated models of Jewish learning and connection that received national recognition and were being piloted in partner cities around the country. But our funding was still overwhelmingly comprised of contributions from our seed funder, along with a few additional individual donors and foundations each contributing $10,000-$50,000/year.

Over lunch with the Millennial donor who had contributed $15,000 to lead Year 3's campaign, he asked me the question that we began this chapter with (and the answer to which you've been brainstorming this whole time):

"I'd like to make a $25,000 investment in your work this year. Now, how can we best leverage those dollars in order to raise additional ones for the organization?"

After brainstorming over lunch and checking in with my team, we decided that we would strive to leverage the $25,000 investment in two ways:

First, we would use the $25,000 as a challenge grant to line up 25 $1,000 donations from young adults/couples excited about our work and capable of investing at that level, who we'd refer to as our "Champions."

Second, we'd use that $50,000 to create a 2:1 match to raise an additional $25,000 from the rest of our participants, with a total campaign goal of $75,000, doubling our participant contributions year-over-year.

One of my mentors continually reminds me that fundraising is not being a nuisance—it's providing people with the opportunity to align their wallets with their values. So, with that sentiment in mind, we compiled a list of those who we knew (a) cared about and/or had been actively engaged with The Well, and (b) who we thought had the capacity to invest $1,000. The list had 75 names on it. In the following two weeks, I made asks. (I was going under the knife to replace the ACL in my knee at the end of the two weeks and set a goal of lining up the 25 $1,000 gifts before the anesthesia kicked in!)

In that two-week period, from the list of 75 potential investors, we lined up 38 young adults/couples to invest at the $1,000 level. In our mid-sized Metro Detroit Jewish community, $1,000 is a significant amount of money— especially for Millennials, who as we established earlier in this chapter generally don't have the disposable income their parents did at a similar age, and whose average annual philanthropic investment is under $500. Let alone that the Jewish community often perceives Millennials as unwilling to invest in its organizations. It was incredibly humbling to see such a positive response.

Relationships played a key role in determining who we invited to be our inaugural Champions. A handful of those we asked hadn't been active Well participants, but had the financial means, an appreciation for the work we were doing in the community, and a personal relationship with me, and thus were happy to invest when asked. Most of our Champions, however, were active Well participants who were excited to invest in the community they were part of and benefiting from. In the pitch, we expressed our commitment to showing our Champions how much we appreciated their support through public acknowledgement, special gatherings, early access to purchase tickets to space-limited gatherings, and more.

What struck me about the asking experience was that even those who said "I can't do $1,000 at this time, I'm sorry" all still invested;

the result was that by virtue of being asked to invest at the $1,000 level, their investments jumped remarkably year-over-year, with many climbing from $36 to $180, from $180 to $360, etc. Whether due to flattery, ego, or the pitch, when asked to give an amount larger than originally planned, people stretched.

With our 38 Champion-level commitments in hand, we prepared for our second annual three-day #BuildTheWell crowdfunding campaign the next month, now able to advertise a 2:1 match to the rest of our participants. I admittedly was concerned we wouldn't hit our $25,000 goal, given that we had secured $13,000 more than we originally anticipated when conceiving of the two-stage campaign courtesy of lining up 38 rather than 25 $1,000 donors. But with our plan in place, we dove in.

At the end of the three days, our team had secured an additional $37,000 from more than 350 Millennial donors, the overwhelming majority of whom were responding to personal asks. This wasn't a "reply to an email solicitation" campaign. This was us using our donor roster from the year before as well as our active participant roster and empowering our lay leaders to reach out to those on the lists they had close personal relationships with to invite them to invest. In addition to the $100,000 total raised from Millennials, we also received roughly $17,000 from parents, grandparents, and more senior community leaders during the three-day campaign, pushing our total to just over $117,000.

What made this campaign different than others? We embraced the concept of inviting Millennials to invest in the community we were building together, and we then made it a point to say thank you creatively.

Names on Walls

In one of my favorite episodes of *Curb Your Enthusiasm*,[230] Larry David learns that Ted Danson made an "anonymous" donation, and yet somehow everyone seems to know that it was Danson who made it and is lavishing praise on him for having done so anonymously. Larry initially is jealous of Danson, but thinks it's a genius plan to donate anonymously and then tell everyone that you're the anonymous donor, soaking up all the *kavod* (honor). Of course, at the subsequent benefit dinner for the charity where Larry has donated anonymously, Larry gets locked out of the building, and when trying to convince the security guard to let him back in, he can't show his name on the wall as proof that he belongs inside, as he has no way of proving that he's "Anonymous."

One need only to look around at our communal buildings to see that donors in the Jewish community have for quite some time been excited about putting their names (and/or those of their loves ones) up on walls. We have a bit of an "edifice complex" as a community in general, loving our physical structures. And we also seem to have a love affair with putting donors' names on them.

Maimonides, the great medieval rabbi, physician and philosopher, taught that one of the most aspirational forms of *tzedakah* (righteous giving) is giving anonymously.[231] So too, we learn in the Talmud:

"Rabbi Elazar said: One who performs *tzedakah* in secret is greater than Moses, our teacher."[232]

And yet, we have this practice in our community of putting donor names on walls. Lest you think this is a newer phenomenon in the course of Jewish history, according to Rabbi Professor David Golinkin, "Normative Jewish practice for some 2,200 years has been to

---

[230] *Curb Your Enthusiasm*, Season 6, Episode 2
[231] Maimonides, Mishnah Torah, Gifts to the Poor 10.
[232] Babylonian Talmud, Bava Batra, Folio 9b.

record gifts and to inscribe the names of donors because this serves as a memorial to the donor and encourages others to give *tzedakah*."[233]

These names on walls have caused problems over the years, as several organizations that realistically should have downsized, merged, relocated or closed their doors haven't done so due to concerns about alienating the donors and their families whose names adorn their facility's walls. I understand the desire for legacy, wanting our names and the names of our loved ones to outlive us and be remembered. At the same time, putting names on physical structures isn't helping our organizations make the strategic decisions they need to. I'd like to propose that going forward, a donor who wants their name to go on a wall can only have it appear there for 20 years—a generation. Almost like stadium naming rights for sports teams, there can be a 20-year agreement, but then the opportunity should exist for another entity to assume those rights or for the organization to decide that their facility no longer meets their strategic needs and to make a change without having to worry about alienating their donors. I'm admittedly not entirely sure how to roll out such a strategic change for those whose names already adorn our community's walls. But going forward we can make an intentional change and emphasize endowing staff positions or particular programs as opposed to being so focused on our buildings.

For a Millennial generation that generally doesn't have the means at this stage to make transformational donations and that doesn't regularly frequent the community's existing physical structures, we decided to use the wall they engage with most frequently to express our gratitude: their Facebook wall.[234] Every single young adult do-

---

[233] David Golinkin, "Is There a Problem with Plaques?" *Responsa in a Moment*, Vol. 2, No. 5, Feb. 2008.www.schechter.edu/is-there-a-problem-with-plaques-responsa-in-a-moment-volume-2-issue-no-5-february-2008.

[234] Admittedly, Facebook isn't necessarily the best place to find Millennials anymore, as along with Gen Z many have gravitated toward Instagram, TikTok, Snapchat and other social media sites. But social media gratitude shout-outs are still important! For more insight on the timeline of Millennial social media migration, see Bianca Bosker, "Teens Are Leaving

nor, regardless of their donation amount, received a personalized shout-out post on Facebook expressing our gratitude and saying kind things about them. This wasn't a generic "Thanks so much for your donation!" post. Instead, they looked more like this:

> "Sam is such an amazing human being. She is a joy to spend time with, lights up the room, leads selflessly, and truly models how to be both an attentive partner and loving parent to a newborn. We are so grateful to be in community with her and are humbled to have her support as we #BuildTheWell."

We had a team of folks making these posts as donations came in, often relying on the person who knew the person best to make the gratitude post. It was a great way to empower and engage lay leaders and our board!

Psychologically, there's no question we love having others say nice things about us—and to have those nice things expressed publicly makes us feel even better. There were fewer than five donors who asked that we refrain from a public Facebook post, preferring their investment be anonymous (Ted Danson would be proud). Even more importantly, based on the power of peer influence as discussed earlier in this chapter, we heard from several people who said they had donated because they saw the public gratitude posts all over their Facebook newsfeeds and wanted to see what nice things our team would say about them publicly after they donated.

A common fundraising strategy used to build relationships with donors is for organizations to have at least seven touchpoints before asking for a subsequent gift.[235] These touchpoints can range from

---

Facebook for Facebook." *The Huffington Post*, 11 Apr. 2014. www.huffpost.com/entry/teens-facebook_n_5127455
[235] Vicki Burkhart, "The Rule of 7: You'll Thank Me For It." The More Than Giving Company. www.morethangiving.co/blog/therule-of-7-youll-thank-me-for-it.

thank-you notes, to birthday calls, to personal invitations to events, and more. So in addition to the public Facebook posts, we proceeded to hand-write and personalize over 400 thank-you notes for each donor—a great way to show appreciation while also empowering our lay and professional team, and simultaneously getting a "touch" in. And believe it or not, despite a love of all things digital, there is nothing Millennials like more than receiving physical mail that is not a bill or an ask for money! In fact, 75% of Millennials said in a 2018 study done by the United States Postal Service Office of the Inspector General that receiving personal mail makes them feel special.[236]

I understand that at The Well's size, dealing with only 400-ish donors, the ability existed to put the personal touch on things in a way that might be harder for larger organizations with larger donor rosters to replicate. As my friend Gary Wolff, the former COO of the Jewish Federation of Greater Dallas says, "strategy and structure have to meet." That said, I'd argue that making our large organizations feel smaller and making each individual donor feel special and appreciated regardless of their investment amount is going to be a key to success with Millennials, who overwhelmingly are not going to invest or donate out of a sense of obligation as previous generations often did and still do.

Admittedly this can be challenging as the time and attention it takes to cultivate and retain "major donors" is significant. And on small teams like ours, figuring out how to keep our Champions engaged while simultaneously cultivating new ones took a lot of time and effort. In Year 5, during our third #BuildTheWell campaign, we were able to replicate our Year 4 success using the same two-tiered model. Of our 38 Champions, 8 declined to reinvest at the $1,000 level (although all made meaningful investments), but we were able

---

[236] "Millennials and the Mail." Office of Inspector General, United States Postal Service. Report Number RARC-WP-18-011. July 30, 2018. www.uspsoig.gov/sites/default/files/reports/2023-01/RARC-WP-18-011.pdf, 6.

to bring on 8 new Champions to take their place. And once again, we raised north of $100,000 from over 400 Millennial donors.

For an organization exclusively serving Millennials in a mid-sized rust belt community, garnering $100,000 in support from more than 400 of our participants in back-to-back years was an incredible accomplishment. With an annual organizational budget at the time of $400,000, to know that a quarter of it was being covered by our participants was on the one hand incredible, as it set us far ahead of most other similarly situated organizations nationally. On the other hand it was very humbling, as the other three quarters of our budget—and thus our existence—truly relied on the good will and investments of larger-scale donors and foundations.

From Detroit to Miami

Lest you think that this model worked exclusively in Metro Detroit and with Millennials, we piloted a version of this campaign model in Miami at the Alper JCC during my year as CEO there as well. The Alper JCC, despite having an over 30-year history, had no regular invitation to those who loved and had benefited from the organization to invest in it. Despite an annual budget north of $7 million, the agency did not have an annual campaign, relying instead on a generous allocation from the Greater Miami Jewish Federation, a few small fundraising events throughout the year, and functioned overwhelmingly as a fee-for-service institution. Could a Legacy Organization in Miami that serves an intergenerational population adopt The Well's multi-day crowdfunding campaign approach and find similar success? You bet.

We chose to organize around The Miami Foundation's "Give Miami Day," where The Miami Foundation ups all contributions with a 6% bump. Since there was no history of an annual campaign, we aimed for breadth over depth just as we did in our first year at The Well so that we could begin to compile an organizational donor roster. We set a goal of 360 donors over a 4-day campaign, which felt like a big, hairy, audacious goal, as this was not even a year into Covid and the world and people's household finances were in a very uncertain place.

Some of the Alper JCC campaign practices adopted from The Well included:

1. Crafting a 2-month deadlines calendar leading up to the campaign
2. Having the 4 days mapped out, in terms of scheduled social media posts across platforms, emails, volunteer times, language to easily have board members copy and paste into email, text, Facebook and phone messages, etc.
3. Lining up social media ambassadors who received texts inviting them to Like, Comment, and Share select posts during the 4 days in order to help give them a "boost" across social media platforms
4. Recording and editing video testimonials from participants to be shared during the campaign
5. Posting personalized messages of gratitude to Facebook for each donation that came in if a personal relationship existed with one of our staff, volunteers or board members
6. Preparing personalized, handwritten Thank You notes for every single donor

In addition, four tactics specifically well-suited to a Legacy Organization serving an intergenerational population (some of whom are less comfortable with social media) were used that would not have been possible at The Well:

We spent weeks compiling spreadsheets of former members, campers, nursery schoolers and the like, datamining as best we could, ultimately producing a list of thousands of potential donors to reach out to.

We signed up with a "text to give" company in order to make giving as easy as possible, because unlike The Well, the Alper JCC kept records of cellphone numbers.

We invited staff and ambassadors who had grown up at the JCC to post photos of themselves with the individuals they were thanking on social media whenever possible, brightening up newsfeeds and playing hard on the nostalgia factor—reminding folks that even if they weren't using the JCC's services now, they had benefitted from them in the past.

We made sure to have volunteers and staff make a significant number of phone calls to potential donors who may not have been users of social media or email, inviting them to invest as well.

Also important was finding ways to have fun! As we hit 270 donations on Day 3, I took a camp-style whipped cream pie to the face for all to see. Once we hit our target of 360 donors on the afternoon of Day 4, several staff (and the president of the board!) joined me and jumped into the pool with our clothes on.

In the end, over four days, using The Well's crowdfunding approach and adapting it modestly to meet the needs of a Legacy Organization, the Alper JCC secured 463 donations—well surpassing our initial goal. After months of managing crises, furloughs and layoffs, Miami becoming the Covid center of the country and more, this was an incredible chance to bring the JCC team together—which we literally did, outdoors, masked, and socially distant—to compose 463 handwritten, personalized thank-you notes the next day.

Interfaith Couples and Charitable Giving

I'm often asked by Jewish Federation leadership teams about the philanthropic tendencies of Millennial interfaith couples, and how to best cultivate and solicit them as donors. For many years, the rallying cry of Federations has been the Talmudic precept of *"Kol Yisrael Arevim Zeh b'Zeh"*—"All of Israel are responsible for one another."[237] The simple truth is that this rallying cry will not resonate with many Millennials, roughly half of whom are the children of interfaith parents,[238] and the majority of whom will marry someone who doesn't happen to be Jewish.

Over 80% of married donors make charitable giving decisions together,[239] so there is a need to understand the philanthropic desires of the non-Jewish partner and to use inclusive language. Those whose immediate family and close friend groups include people who don't happen to be Jewish will inevitably question the particularistic nature of the *"Kol Yisrael"* pitch, instead preferring to support organizations that deliver services to people of all backgrounds. My recommendation is to tailor the pitch to those you're courting. If you're trying to entice interfaith couples to donate to your Federation's annual campaign, when pulling statistics and fun facts to share, emphasize that your Federation is the local Jewish community's central vehicle for *Tikkun Olam*—repairing the world.

Many local Federation beneficiary agencies such as Jewish Community Centers serve significant numbers of people who don't happen to be Jewish, but our Federations haven't been in the habit of trumpeting that fact due to concerns about alienating Traditionalist and Baby Boomer donors. In most communities, a meaningful portion of the Federation's annual campaign is allocated to their "Israel and Overseas" department, with those dollars generally supporting The Jewish Agency for Israel (JAFI) and the American Jewish Joint

---

[237] Babylonian Talmud, Shevuot, Folio 39a. "Israel" in this construct refers to the Children of Israel—i.e., "the Jewish people."

[238] Sasson, Theodore, et al., "Millennial Children of Intermarriage." Brandeis University, 2015. http://bir.brandeis.edu/bitstream/handle/10192/31190/MillennialChildrenIntermarriage1.pdf, 5.

[239] "How Couples Give." Fidelity Charitable, 2017. www.fidelitycharitable.org/content/dam/fc-public/docs/insights/how-couples-give.pdf.

Distribution Committee (JDC). But why not highlight that JAFI has designated programs intended to support Israel's non-Jewish citizens[240] while the JDC has a disaster relief department that helps folks around the world regardless of their religious background?[241] Framing a Federation gift as contributing toward the Jewish project of repairing the world—for all of its inhabitants—while at the same time making sure the specific needs of the Jewish people are met is a compelling way to frame federated giving for Millennial interfaith couples. It's a framing that will also work well for Millennials in general, who we know tend to be universalistic in their outlook.[242]

Core Takeaways

1. As with all philanthropy, relationship cultivation with Millennials is key, and personal outreach from someone in meaningful relationship with the potential donor is essential.

2. Millennials are philanthropic and are ready and excited to invest in organizations whose missions they care about and/or feel that they are personally benefitting from (or have benefitted from), and whose leadership is transparent.

3. Challenges and match opportunities are generally well received, with much room for creativity. Peer invitations (and pressure) are powerful and can be used to inspire giving.

4. When asked to invest a reach amount, Millennials will likely give more than they originally anticipated giving, even if they don't give the requested amount.

---

[240] Sam Sokol, "For Jewish Agency, Israeli Arabs an increasing priority." *The Jerusalem Post*, Feb. 21, 2016. www.jpost.com/israel-news/for-jewish-agency-israeli-arabs-an-increasing-priority-445642.

[241] "JDC Disaster Response." JDC. www.jdc.org/disasters/.

[242] Shlomi Ravid, "Engaging Millennials with Jewish Peoplehood." Center for Jewish Peoplehood Education, 2016. www.jpeoplehood.org/wp-content/uploads/2016/06/Peoplehood17-updated.pdf, 4.

5. Gratitude is key. Finding ways to say thank you repeatedly, regardless of the amount invested (and meaning it!), is essential. There are so many ways people can spend their dollars. Whether someone donates $5 or $1,000, it's important we shower gratitude and celebrate them. It makes giving feel good and inspires more!

6. Millennials want to know their investment has made a difference. Be sure to communicate with them actively how their investment dollars were used and the impact they had.

7. Don't be shy about differentiating your pitch when pitching to distinct audiences. A tailored, targeted message is more powerful than a generic one.

Discussion Questions

- What assumptions does our organization make when it comes to Millennials and philanthropy?
- Are we better classified as a charity or an investment in the Millennial mind, and how can we tailor our pitch accordingly?
- Are we saying thank you to our supporters at least 7 times between asks? If not, why not?
- How long do our campaigns generally last? What would it look like to shorten them to add a sense of urgency?
- What naming opportunities exist for our organization beyond putting names on physical walls?
- Are we effectively tailoring our pitch to our intended audiences?

Chapter 8

The Remixed Beit Midrash

This is Torah, and I must learn.
—Babylonian Talmud, Berachot, Folio 62a

I remember the moment I fell in love with Jewish wisdom as an adult. I was in my early 20s, studying with my rabbi and a group of friends after Shabbat services one morning. We were examining a section of the Talmud that dealt with when it was appropriate to interrupt one's intense study in the Beit Midrash (House of Study). And we came across the following text:

> This was also taught: The house of Rabban Gamliel would not say "*marpeh*" in the study hall, because it would be negating the study hall.[243]

In more easily understandable terms: just how important is it to be focused on studying while in the House of Study? It's so important that Rabban Gamliel and his students wouldn't even say *marpeh*. And what on earth does *marpeh* mean? It's the equivalent of *salud*, *livruit*, or my personal favorite, *gezundheit*. The word literally means "health," and it's what you say after someone sneezes!

This moment for me was connective in a deep way, not because I was impressed that Rabban Gamliel and his crew were so laser-focused on study that they couldn't bother wishing someone else good health, but because it was the first time I truly realized that I was genuinely connected to these folks who lived 1,500+ years ago— my ancestors, who, like me, also said *gezundheit* or its equivalent

[243] Babylonian Talmud, Berachot, Folio 53a.

when people sneezed! People have been saying "to your health" when someone sneezes for over 1,500 years! That's amazing! That realization completely humanized the text to me, made it feel contemporarily relevant as opposed to archaic, and led to my desire to continue studying our sacred texts.

We learned from the 2013 Pew Research Study of American Jews that 94% of American Jewish adults are proud to be Jewish.[244] But how many have had such an "aha" moment? How many of them post-Bar/Bat/B-mitzvah, if they celebrated at all, have chosen to dive into our inherited wisdom, to see all it can offer in terms of living a full, purpose-driven life that allows one to flourish individually while living as part of an intentional and committed community? What exactly about being Jewish are they proud of? How many of these proud folks have any Jewish content knowledge or understanding of Jewish values beyond phrases like *"Tikkun Olam"* (colloquially, "repairing the world") and "be a good person"—two statements that just as easily could have been expressed by Mother Theresa, of blessed memory?

Mother Theresa taught:

> "I want you to be concerned about your next-door neighbor. Do you know your next-door neighbor?"[245]

Rabbi Akiva said:

> "'You shall love your neighbor as yourself' is a great principle of the Torah."[246]

Loving our neighbors as ourselves—being concerned about their wellbeing—is indeed a core Jewish value. But it's not unique to Ju-

---

[244] "Highlights of the Pew Research Center's 2013 Survey of U.S. Jews." The Berman Jewish Databank, Oct. 1, 2013. www.jewishdatabank.org/content/upload/bjdb/715/DataBank%20Slides_2013%20Pew%20Center%20Survey%20of%20U.S.%20Jews.pdf, "Attitudes" slide.
[245] Mother Theresa, *No Greater Love* (New World Library, 2002), 27.
[246] Sifra, Kedoshim, 4:12

daism. Repairing our broken world has become a contemporary rallying cry, rooted in the philosophy of 16th-century Kabbalist Rabbi Isaac Luria, whose mystical teachings led to what we think of as our responsibility for healing a fractured world. Embracing both core approaches to life may indeed instill pride in being Jewish. But is pride, absent any sort of additional substantive content knowledge, really a sufficient 21st-century communal outcome given the time, effort, energy, and massive amounts of philanthropy invested in Jewish education, engagement, identity development and the like?

Let's be real: your average Jewish Millennial maybe had a Bar/Bat/B-Mitzvah after some sort of preparatory course of study or Hebrew School experience, and even if they did that likely was the end of their formal Jewish learning journey.[247] Drop-off rates in Jewish learning experiences post Bar/Bat/B-mitzvah are well documented,[248] with a modest number engaged in Jewish youth groups (which lean toward the purely social), some getting involved with Hillel on campus, maybe going on a Birthright trip while in college, and then often nothing. As a result, Jewish Millennials have overwhelmingly never been exposed to the adult content of our tradition! There are certain things we simply don't share or talk about with 13-year-olds, as to do so would be inappropriate (the Song of Songs—the erotic poetry section of the Hebrew Bible—comes to mind...).

Holding back pieces of the Tradition from those who aren't "ready" to be exposed to it has strong roots. We read in the Mishnah:

He [Judah ben Tema] used to say: At five years of age
the study of Scripture; At ten the study of Mishnah;
At thirteen subject to the commandments; At fifteen

---

[247] "Jewish Americans in 2020." Pew Research Center, May 11, 2021. www.pewresearch.org/religion/wp-content/uploads/sites/7/2021/05/PF_05.11.21_Jewish.Americans.pdf, 108.
[248] "The drop-out phenomenon after Bar/Bat Mitzvah is dramatic. More than one-third of students drop out after grade 7 and then the rate of decline accelerates so that by grade 12 only one-seventh of the number of seventh graders is still enrolled." Jack Wertheimer, "A Census of Jewish Supplementary Schools In The United States." The AVI CHAI Foundation, 2008. www.avichai.org/wp-content/uploads/2010/06/Supplementary-School-Census-Report-Final.pdf, 3.

the study of Talmud; At eighteen the bridal canopy;
At twenty for pursuit [of livelihood]; At thirty the
peak of strength; At forty wisdom; At fifty able to
give counsel; At sixty old age; At seventy fullness
of years; At eighty the age of "strength"; At ninety
a bent body; At one hundred, as good as dead and
gone completely out of the world.[249]

Here we find Judah ben Tema teaching that different ages and life stages are associated with learning different content. Of note, he highlights "wisdom" as being something one begins to attain at age 40, which is why *Kabbalah* (Jewish mysticism) historically wasn't taught until married men turned 40 years old. But due to not being exposed to the fullness of our tradition, most Jewish Millennials are walking through the world with a Judaism that is pediatric at best. And even worse, they don't think to look to Judaism when it comes time to find answers to the most fundamental of human questions: Why am I here, and what's my purpose in life? Thus, it's normative for Jewish Millennials to seek out answers to life's big questions elsewhere, never considering that their own inherited tradition might have answers that will speak to them. We need to find ways to expose Jewish Millennials to awesome, fun, challenging, meaningful, and relevant wisdom nuggets of the Jewish tradition, hopefully inspiring them to want to learn more as a result. And ideally to do it in a way that doesn't require us to pay them, as discussed earlier.

So, what is it that's preventing Millennials from studying Jewish texts? Standard responses we might expect include a perceived lack of time, dollars, interest, self-consciousness at their lack of pre-existing knowledge, and more. There may also be assumptions that Judaism is out of touch, or is for kids and has nothing to offer contemporary young adults. But beyond these assumptions, there's a key factor preventing Jewish Millennials from embracing Jewish text

[249] Pirke Avot, 5:21

study that deserves attention, and I call it "The Calculus Questions." What are "The Calculus Questions"? The Calculus Questions are the questions that I asked every single day of calculus class in high school: When am I ever going to use this? And how in any way, shape, or form is this relevant to my life? (Needless to say, Calculus is the only class I ever got a "C" in...) Too frequently we forget to bring relevance into the conversation!

How do we create a model that educates Jewish Millennials about their tradition while simultaneously oozing relevance and inspiring them to want to learn more? My answer is that the model already exists, but that it needs to be remixed. And it's called the Beit Midrash.

What is the Beit Midrash? Literally the "House of Study," think of it as a large study hall with volumes upon volumes of sacred books lining the walls, filled with the glorious cacophony of people reading, discussing, debating, and studying the texts of our people. Admittedly, you may think I'm a bit crazy to suggest the Beit Midrash is the ideal model for Millennial learning today, because the Beit Midrash has existed for thousands of years and during that time has been the primary venue for studying the Jewish canon. We're taught in the Talmud:

> Love the Beit Midrash so that your children may come to study the Torah.[250]

Or, for a bit darker of an approach:

> R. Meir said: Whoever has a Beit Midrash in his town and does not frequent it forfeits his life.[251]

This love for—and intensity of commitment to—the Beit Midrash remains strong, as in addition to observant Orthodox folks for whom the Beit Midrash is often a core component of their lives,

---

[250] Babylonian Talmud, Derekh Eretz Zuta, 9:4
[251] Babylonian Talmud, Derekh Eretz Rabbah, 11:13

there are a number of organizations around the world that are seeking to make the Beit Midrash relevant to a non-Orthodox audience, such as Svara and the Pardes Institute for Jewish Studies. But the overwhelming majority of Jewish Millennials are not stepping foot into them or engaging with the Jewish textual tradition in any regular, meaningful way. Yet the model contains many of the right ingredients, and with some contemporary remixing, creates a fruitful environment for learning.

Thanks to an Ignition Grant from The Covenant Foundation, we were able to pilot and play at The Well as we crystallized the Remixed Beit Midrash model, which we initially called "CSI: Coffee. Study. Interpret.", as we hoped to "investigate" topics and texts of interest and wanted to emphasize that, unlike some other organizations, we were not going to use the allure of free alcohol to try to attract participants. We were going to meet at coffee shops—not bars. After significant experimentation, we landed on the following programmatic outline for each of these gatherings:

1. Welcome and Framing (5 minutes)
2. Set Induction (10 minutes)
3. Small Group Conversations/Text Study (30 minutes)
4. Expert Speaker speaks (20 minutes)
5. Q&A (20 minutes)
6. Wrap Up and Closing Charge (5 minutes)

For two years, we hosted monthly CSI gatherings, packing local coffee houses with Millennials, receiving significant press coverage in both secular and Jewish media. The model was designated a semi-finalist for the inaugural Lippman Kanfer Prize in Applied Jewish Wisdom, and we were fortunate to receive a Signature Grant from The Covenant Foundation, giving us the opportunity to work closely with partner organizations in other cities to help them pilot the model in their communities as well.

Despite what many consider to be a massive investment in Jewish young adult engagement and education by the organized Jewish community, the reality is that very few communities have full-time designated professionals who are working with Millennials specifically. Federations may have a "young adult division" director, but often they don't have additional staff and their focus is overwhelmingly on cultivating donors as opposed to enhancing Jewish literacy. Our expansion proposal to the Covenant Foundation specifically indicated that we were going to seek out partners in comparatively underfunded small to mid-sized communities so that their grant dollars could go further (it's cheaper to rent out a coffee shop in Cleveland than in New York City!), and so that we could have a greater local impact and not get lost in competing noise. And yet, what we found was that outside of the major urban centers where most Jewish Millennials live there is very little infrastructure in place to support the kind of relationship building and programmatic endeavors that Millennials crave and that we were offering. We were committed to cultivating partnerships with organizations in small to mid-size Jewish communities, and we were bringing dollars to the table to help pilot the Remixed Beit Midrash model in them, and what we found was either no full-time professional focused on young adults to partner with or a single individual who was already stretched thin, lacking the capacity or desire to take on an additional project. In the end, we were fortunate to line up partners in Cleveland, Memphis and Baltimore—but it took significantly more effort to identify and secure them than we had originally anticipated.

Courtesy of our experience locally in Detroit, along with our learnings from piloting the model in partner communities, we determined that there are 5 key ingredients to the Remixed Beit Midrash model:

1. Relevance
2. "This Is Torah"
3. Expert Speakers
4. Small Discussion Groups
5. Texts & Framing

Relevance

"That's the problem with religion right now. It hasn't evolved. And instead of being open and looking for ways to be relevant in today's world, it's gone all defensive and protective and it's regressed into lowest-common-denominator sound bites—and fundamentalism."[252]

Let's start with relevance. Traditionally, what is studied in the Beit Midrash is the *Tanakh* (the Hebrew Bible) and associated rabbinic commentaries (some legalistic—*Halakha*—some storytelling—*Aggadah*) spanning the generations. At first glance, some of these texts seem more relevant than others but they are a treasure trove of wisdom, cultural narrative, and more, waiting to be studied and framed in a relevant way! But when thinking about how to inspire Millennials to self-select into coming to study these texts, building gatherings around topics that are already of interest and on their minds is a good place to start.

The first Remixed Beit Midrash hosted by The Well was titled "Lead in the Water" and was focused on the Flint Water Crisis. The next leaned into learning about the Syrian Refugee crisis. And the third was called "Congrats on your gay marriage, you're fired." Other topics over the years included the opioid epidemic, the euthanizing

---

[252] Raymond Khoury, *The Sign* (Berkley, 2010), 33.

of Harambe the gorilla at the Cincinnati Zoo, mass incarceration, regional transit and more—topics that were in the news and already on the minds of Jewish Millennials. These topics may not immediately jump at you as being Jewish in nature, but that's exactly the point. Your average Jewish Millennial doesn't necessarily think the Jewish tradition has anything of value to say on contemporary issues, but they couldn't be more mistaken.

Admittedly, one of the challenges in striving to be relevant by addressing topics that are on peoples' minds is that in today's 24-hour news cycle, it seems there's a roughly 24-48 hour window before the media turns their focus elsewhere, unless it's a slow news week. Trying to select Remixed Beit Midrash topics months as opposed to weeks in advance is therefore challenging. Bringing intention to focusing on topics that will maintain their relevance a few weeks later is an important consideration, so that there's sufficient time to secure a guest speaker, put together a substantive text packet, and more. For many Legacy Organizations, moving quickly is not something that comes naturally or comfortably. It's not uncommon to hear things like, "But our newsletter deadline is 2 months before the event, and we need to have all the details already finalized so that they can be included." If relevance is key, which we know it to be, there needs to be a willingness to plan, communicate, and move quickly, and this might mean that details about the gathering don't make it into the organizational newsletter.

"This Is Torah"

There may be some who argue that only Jewish topics should be covered in the Beit Midrash, and some of the rabbis of the Talmudic era would agree. But there's a particular Talmudic story that speaks to this concern, and provides the rallying cry for the Remixed Beit Midrash:

> The Gemara shares that Rav Kahana entered the bed-
> room and lay beneath his teacher Rav's bed. He heard
> Rav chatting and laughing with his wife and seeing
> to his needs. Rav Kahana said to Rav: Your mouth
> is like one who has never eaten a cooked dish! Rav
> said to him: Kahana, you are here? Leave, as this is
> an undesirable mode of behavior! Rav Kahana said
> to him: This is Torah, and I must learn![253]

What's happening here? Imagine a movie scene, where a rambunctious student sneaks into his teacher's bedroom and hides under the bed. While hiding there, the teacher returns home with his
wife after a night on the town and they proceed to do adult things
on the bed, not knowing the student is hiding beneath it. Amazed
at what he hears coming out of his teacher's mouth, the student
can't help but blurt out the equivalent of "Wow, you're lustful!" The
teacher hears him and responds "Is that you, student? GET OUT of
my bedroom!" And the student responds, "I'm not going anywhere,
because this is Torah, and I need to learn!"

"This is Torah." All human experience—even what goes on in the
bedroom—is Torah, and Judaism has insights and wisdom to offer,
regardless of the topic. After all, the Talmud is full of conversations
about sex, farting, food, travel, prostitution, and more—things that
go far beyond what we might consider holy or even Jewish. Frankly,
sometimes it seems like Talmudic stories may have been the basis
for the Marvel Cinematic Universe, with tales of demigods, people
who shoot laser beams out of their eyes, giants, and more! "This is
Torah" needs to be the rallying cry of the Jewish community... or
at least those within it who are passionate about sharing our textual
tradition with emerging generations. So too, the Remixed Beit Midrash needs to be ready to explore anything and everything that is
on the minds of Millennials.

[253] Babylonian Talmud, Berachot, Folio 62a.

Expert Speakers

For much of Jewish history, rabbis have been the designated "subject matter experts," and in many ways the gatekeepers of Jewish wisdom. Their supremacy was keenly felt not only in the Beit Midrash, but in life in general. We learn in Pirke Avot, the section of the Mishna (the 2nd-century legal code) described as "The Ethics of our Ancestors":

> Yose ben Yoezer used to say: Let your house be a house of meeting for the rabbis, and sit in the very dust of their feet, and drink in their words with thirst.[254]

The rabbis taught that you should open your home to them and soak up all that they had to teach. Even today, in more traditionally observant communities, rabbis regularly field phone calls from their flock who have questions about Jewish life and practice that they're seeking answers to. And to be able to make informed Jewish legal rulings, rabbis often have to become subject-matter experts in a range of topics, including emerging technologies.[255] Think about it: if you don't know how the invention works, you can't really determine whether it fits into a prohibited or permitted category.

But with a shift to a "this too is Torah" mindset, the reality is that rabbis are not necessarily going to be the subject matter experts on every topic—and generally aren't going to be attractive enough of a draw to entice Millennials to attend a particular learning event. Rabbis don't exactly have the street cred today that they may have once had—especially among non-Orthodox, unaffiliated Jewish Millennials. So, for the Remixed Beit Midrash, the opportunity exists to invite expert speakers to present on whatever the designated topic might be for a particular gathering. And, what matters most is

---

[254] Pirke Avot, 1:4
[255] For example: Daniel S. Nevins, "The Use of Electrical and Electronic Devices on Shabbat." The Rabbinical Assembly, May 31, 2012. www.rabbinicalassembly.org/sites/default/files/public/halakhah/teshuvot/2011-2020/electrical-electronic-devices-shabbat.pdf.

their expertise—meaning these speakers need not be Jewish! (Although in our experience, if they are Jewish they might be more willing to speak at a Jewish-sponsored event at a reduced cost or to simply donate their time).

For example, at The Well's Lead in the Water gathering focused on the Flint Water Crisis, the featured presenter was the chief of staff to the state senator from Flint. At the gathering focusing on the euthanizing of Harambe the Gorilla (for those who don't remember, a 3-year-old child fell into Harambe's pen at the Cincinnati Zoo and ultimately Harambe was killed to save the child), the featured presenter was the CEO of the Detroit Zoo, who spoke about the situation, the decision-making calculus involved, and the changing nature of zoos. At the "Congrats on your gay marriage, you're fired" gathering focused on LGBTQ+ rights, the featured presenter was the federal judge who had composed the District Court opinion that was ultimately looped into the Supreme Court's gay marriage decision. And at the event focusing on the Syrian Refugee Crisis, the featured presenters were Syrian refugees who had recently relocated to Detroit who shared their personal stories of strife and survival. Due to welcoming expert presenters on topics that were relevant to Millennials, turnout at each of these gatherings was excellent, and many who had never self-selected to engage in Jewish learning before were now crossing the threshold into the Remixed Beit Midrash.

Small Discussion Groups

But where does the Jewish learning piece fit in, you ask? The relevant academic literature and our applied experience makes clear that Millennials appreciate having the chance to engage in conversation as opposed to attending lengthy lectures. Frankly, it's one reason that intergenerational programming is challenging for many Jewish organizations. A few of our Remixed Beit Midrash offerings were open to the broader community regardless of age, and on post-event feedback surveys, older participants made it very clear that they wanted to hear exclusively from the expert speaker and expressed disinterest in hearing what other program attendees thought during breakout discussion groups. Our Millennial participants on the other hand expressed that a lecture should never last more than 20-30 minutes, and they desired lots of time for processing content and discussing in smaller groups. When curating a Jewish learning gathering for Millennials, in addition to featuring an expert speaker, small group breakout discussions are an essential component.

In the traditional Beit Midrash model, students traditionally split into pairs called *chevruta*—from the root *chaver* meaning "friend." Essentially, everyone has a designated holy study buddy. For many people this model of having a special person in your life whom you study Torah with is working. The rabbinic tradition places great emphasis on having a *chevruta*:

> Rabbi Hama, son of Rabbi Hanina, said: Why is it written: "Iron sharpens iron…" (Proverbs 27:17)? To teach you that just as with iron implements one sharpens the other, so too, Torah scholars sharpen one another in matters of *halakha*.[256]

Studying by oneself is thoroughly frowned upon by the rabbis of the Talmud, who emphasize that a core value in having a study buddy is so that you can help enhance each other's understanding of the various texts and associated laws.

However, for those who have little to no background in studying Jewish texts and are attending a larger community gathering, to break off into pairs with a stranger—as opposed to someone you've established a study buddy relationship with—can be incredibly in-

---

[256] Babylonian Talmud, Taanit, Folio 7a.

timidating. To alleviate anxieties and ensure that no single voice dominated a pairing, we experimented with small groups of 3-6 people and received constant feedback indicating that the small group model worked best to encourage reflection, sharing, questioning, and more. This small group discussion model is used effectively in many settings, from primary schools to Harvard Law School:

> "Now I like to have students talk to their neighbors first before talking with the whole class about a problem like that. It gets everybody's mind thinking. It gets everybody in the class participating, and trying to be active. That's a tremendous amount of education going on and [that] students are getting from each other. And it is a way that you can bring the benefits of participating in class to people who are shy or otherwise don't participate very much in class. They spent 15-20 minutes actively participating, even though only two other people heard what they had to say."[257]

In addition, just as you might find a learned person roaming the floors of the traditional Beit Midrash to help answer questions that might arise, there is value in having rabbis or other trained educators (or empowered peers) circulate among the various groups during these breakout conversations in order to help answer questions that might arise, offer points of clarification if needed, and to help steer discussions in productive ways if necessary.

---

[257] Todd Rakoff, "Getting students thinking and engaging through small-group discussion." Harvard Graduate School of Education. https://instructionalmoves.gse.harvard.edu/getting-students-thinking-and-engaging-through-small-group-discussion.

Texts & Framing

Textual selections from our tradition now become the vehicle, accompanied by guiding discussion questions, to spark conversation in these small breakout groups. For example, the text packet for the Harambe the Gorilla gathering included the following selection from the Torah:

> Then the servant took ten of his master's camels and set out, taking with him all the bounty of his master; and he made his way to Aram-naharaim, to the city of Nahor. He made the camels kneel down by the well outside the city, at evening time, the time when women come out to draw water. And he said, "God of my master Abraham, grant me good fortune this day, and deal graciously with my master Abraham: Here I stand by the spring as the daughters of the townsmen come out to draw water; let the maiden to whom I say, 'Please, lower your jar that I may drink,' and who replies, 'Drink, and I will also water your camels'—let her be the one whom You have decreed for Your servant Isaac. Thereby shall I know that You have dealt graciously with my master.[258]

Eliezer, Abraham's servant, travels to find a wife for Isaac at Abraham's instruction. He asks for a sign from God—a woman who'll not only offer him water but will offer to water his 10 camels as well. Lo and behold, almost immediately after he expresses this desire, Rebecca appears and does exactly that:

> The servant ran toward her and said, "Please, let me sip a little water from your jar." "Drink, my lord," she

---

[258] Genesis 24:10-14.

said, and she quickly lowered her jar upon her hand and let him drink. When she had let him drink his fill, she said, "I will also draw for your camels, until they finish drinking." Quickly emptying her jar into the trough, she ran back to the well to draw, and she drew for all his camels.[259]

The discussion question that accompanied this text, at a gathering focused on humanity's relationship with the animal kingdom, was:

Is kindness to animals something you look(ed) for in a romantic partner? Why or why not?

It's a simple question, and it frames the Torah text in a way that is immediately relatable to a Millennial audience—one that is over-whelmingly comprised of those seeking or who have recently found their "person."[260] When I shared this piece of Torah and the accompanying question with my mother, she shared that the moment she knew my father was the man for her was when he got down on his hands and knees and played with her family dog the first time he visited her home!

Jewish texts, with thoughtful framing, can spark meaningful conversations and speak to the things Millennials care about. But while you might think that a text packet used in this kind of environment should include exclusively Jewish texts, you'd be wrong. In the Re-mixed Beit Midrash, Jewish texts alone, absent framing, will not scream "relevant" to this generation. There is room for poetry, selections from other wisdom traditions, academic and newspaper articles, and more.

---

[259] Genesis 24:17-20.

[260] Fun fact: the term "my person" used in this way (connoting one's soul mate) was popularized by Jewish character Dr. Christina Yang on the popular television show Grey's Anatomy. See also: Lisa Bonos, "'You're my person': How 'Grey's Anatomy' created a stand-in for 'soul mate.'" *The Washington Post*, Dec. 4, 2018. www.washingtonpost.com/lifestyle/2018/12/04/youre-my-person-how-greys-anatomy-created-stand-in-soul-mate.

For example, at a Remixed Beit Midrash gathering titled "The Plague of Mass Incarceration," timed to take place just before the Passover holiday (which commemorates the liberation of the Israelites from slavery in Egypt), the text packet included teachings ranging from the medieval rabbinic sage Maimonides to selections from Michelle Alexander's book *The New Jim Crow*. And I'll never forget 24-year-old Hayley, encountering these texts and their interplay for the first time, shouting from the back of the room: "F*ck Yeah, Torah!" The words speak for themselves. The expletive translates to, "Holy smokes! My tradition has something relevant to say about the things I care about, and I never thought to delve into it! Teach me more!"

There are some who might worry that by including textual selections from beyond the traditional Jewish canon, that somehow the Jewish learning is being diluted. As I mentioned earlier, there are rabbinic positions that suggest that studying anything other than the Jewish canon (colloquially "Torah"), is a waste of one's time. In the Talmud, we find the following:

> Rabbi Nehorai says: Anyone for whom it is possible to engage in Torah study and who nevertheless does not engage in its study is included in the category of: "Because he has despised the word of God."[261]

Rabbi Nehorai's position, along with others, serves as a foundation for the concept of *bitul Torah*—negating Torah study. The argument is essentially that since Torah study is meant to be something Jewish people do continuously when possible, it's inherently wrong to do anything else with our time—like reading newspaper articles, secular poetry, works of fiction, etc. To such traditionalists, I'd respectfully counter with the "this too is Torah" framework and emphasize that framing particularistic Jewish wisdom as part

---

[261] Babylonian Talmud, Sanhedrin, Folio 99a.

of broader universal human wisdom, and showing how the Jewish tradition is in conversation with the sources, real-world experiences, and people the average Jewish Millennial is, doesn't dilute the Jewish content or tradition—rather, it helps it root more deeply in the learner, and capably meets the definition of studying Torah.

The gathering focusing on the Syrian Refugee Crisis is what first attracted Alyah Al-Azem to The Well (she eventually became a board member). She writes that at the gathering, "We heard the personal stories of two Syrian refugees currently residing in Michigan and the struggles they and their families went through to make it here. We also engaged in conversations using text as a jump-off point—including selections from Emma Lazarus, Tony Kusher, Torah, Talmud, Maimonides, and contemporary Syrian rap lyrics. The major takeaway from the gathering? Syrian refugees are human beings, and as Jews, we have the obligation to act in some meaningful way—we cannot stand idly by. I was moved."[262]

The Jewish tradition has much to say about the world we live in. When framed and presented properly, it will without question resonate with Millennials, who will walk away saying, "This is Torah, and I must learn."

[262] Alyah Al-Azem. "How a Discussion on Syrian Refugees Brought Me Back to Communal Judaism." *Forward*, Aug. 24, 2016. www.forward.com/community/348406/how-a-discussion-on-syrian-refugees-brought-me-back-to-communal-judaism.

Core Takeaways

1. Remember the 5 core ingredients to inspiring Millennials to participate in Jewish learning:
   1. Relevance
   2. "This Is Torah"
   3. Expert Speakers
   4. Small Discussion Groups
   5. Texts & Framing
2. As with everything, co-creation is the name of the game. Don't just pick a topic and try to attract folks top-down. Rather, assemble a group of Millennials and ask them what's on their minds. Actively listen. Share with them the Remixed Beit Midrash model and invite them to co-create with you. Reach out to partner organizations of interest and invite them to be part of the process.
3. Remember: Third Places tend to attract Millennials more than Legacy Organization structures. Reserve a quality venue that meets your needs and best allows you to achieve your programmatic goals.
4. Book an expert speaker, who doesn't need to be Jewish and certainly doesn't need to be a rabbi.
5. Include diverse sources and guiding discussion questions in your text packet. Depending on organizational capacity, this can be outsourced to a local rabbi or Jewish educator.
6. Plan the gathering for 90 minutes max. It keeps things flowing, leaves people wanting more, and gives permission to those who want or need to leave to head out, while creating the space for others to stay and continue discussing if they wish to.

Discussion Questions

- How does our organization infuse its existing offerings with substantive Jewish content?
- Are we bringing intention to framing Jewish wisdom as contemporarily relevant? If so, how so? If not, why not?
- How does our organization define what makes something "Jewish"? Are we able to embrace an expansive "This is Torah" construct?
- What are other models rooted in tradition that could be reimagined to meet our needs today?
- Did you notice this chapter included textual selections both Jewish and secular to help frame the topic?

chapter 9

Getting Rid of (the word) God

*I Adonai am your God who brought you out of the land of Egypt,
the house of bondage: You shall have no other gods besides Me.*
—*Exodus 20:2-3*

One of my favorite jokes (it's a classic) goes something like this:

A young boy is confused about why his outspoken atheist father
goes to synagogue prayer services every Shabbat morning. He asks:
"Dad, why do you go to synagogue if you don't believe in God?" His
father replies: "Well, you know my friend Goldberg? Goldberg goes
to synagogue every week to talk to God. And I go to synagogue to
talk to Goldberg!"

While a majority of American adults (56%) say they believe in
God "as described in the Bible," only about a quarter of U.S. Jews
express such a belief (26%). American Jews are more likely to believe in some other kind of higher power or in no higher power at
all.[263] This especially holds true for Millennials, 60% of whom would
rather express their faith by talking to their friends than by attending
synagogue.[264] One of the primary arenas of Jewish life where God is
invoked regularly is in our prayer services. So it should come as no
surprise that the overwhelming majority of Jewish Millennials are
not regularly participating in synagogue prayer services, and if they
do at all, that it's on the High Holidays of Rosh Hashanah and Yom

---

[263] "Jewish Americans in 2020." Pew Research Center, May 11, 2021. www.pewresearch.org/
religion/wp-content/uploads/sites/7/2021/05/PF_05.11.21_Jewish.Americans.pdf, 22.
[264] Anna Greenberg, "OMG! How Generation Y is Redefining Faith In The iPod Era." *Reboot*,
Apr. 2005. www.yumpu.com/en/document/read/28072223/omg-how-generation-y-is-
redefining-faith-in-the-ipod-era-circle, 11.

Kippur.[265] Anecdotally, I'd wager that their attendance has as much to do with fulfilling a sense of familial obligation (whether for their parents or their children) as it does with seeking a spiritual connection. While God is a core focus of Jewish life for most traditionally observant Jews, that isn't the case for the overwhelming majority of non-Orthodox Millennial Jews.

Traditionally observant Jews pray three times a day, every day. This practice mimics the thrice daily sacrifices that were offered at the Temple when it stood in Jerusalem. When the Temple was destroyed by the Romans in 70 CE,[266] the rabbis instituted prayer as the replacement for sacrifices.[267] As a result, for almost two millennia, praying three times each day has been considered a *mitzvah* (plural: *mitzvot*)—an obligatory commandment.[268] But as Rabbi Harold Schulweis (of blessed memory) taught, "Most people don't pray, not in the synagogue, not at home, not on the golf course, except for a divine expletive or in response to a sneeze— '*gesundheit.*' God bless you."[269]

Classical Jewish theology understands the Torah to have been given by God to Moses at Mt. Sinai,[270] resulting in a special covenant with the Israelites in which they commit to observing the *mitzvot*. However, post-Enlightenment, and in an era of broad assimilation, most Jewish Millennials don't read the Torah's narrative as factual or

---

[265] "Jewish Americans in 2020," 80.

[266] CE stands for "Common Era." Customarily, Jews avoid using AD and BC due to their direct linkage to Christianity, and instead use BCE ("Before Common Era") and CE ("Common Era") in their place.

[267] "Rabbi Yehoshua ben Levi said that the prayers were instituted based on the daily offerings sacrificed in the Holy Temple, and the prayers parallel the offerings, in terms of both time and characteristics…" Babylonian Talmud, Berakhot, Folio 26b.

[268] *Mitzvah* is commonly mistranslated as "good deed" instead of "commandment." Some *mitzvot* are indeed what we might contemporarily consider good deeds, such as visiting the sick. Others, such as stoning rebellious children and slaughtering anyone who's a descendent of the Amalekite nation, are a bit more complicated.

[269] Harold Schulweis, "Is Prayer Magic?" Valley Beth Shalom. www.vbs.org/worship/meet-our-clergy/rabbi-harold-schulweis/sermons/prayer-magic.

[270] As told in Exodus chapters 19 and 20.

historical, and don't believe in a God who—in the past or current-ly—actively communicates with people.[271] As a result, most Mil-lennials don't view themselves as divinely obligated to fulfill *mitzvot*, such as praying daily. And yet, if you look at the *siddurim* (prayer books) of most major Jewish denominations, you find constant ref-erences to an omnipotent[272] and omniscient[273] God; theologies that simply don't resonate with Millennials.

When Jews who do not attend religious services regularly are asked why they don't attend more often, the most offered response is "I'm not religious."[274] Among Jews who do attend religious ser-vices regularly, about 9 out of 10 say they do so because they find it spiritually meaningful.[275] Notice that it's not because they under-stand themselves as commanded to do so. Outside of theologically embracing a covenantal construct that includes commandedness, the primary reason a Millennial is going to do anything Jewish is because they find personal meaning in it.

We live in an era in which Jews have been embraced throughout American society. Professor Jack Wertheimer teaches that as a result, we are all "Jews by choice"[276] (a moniker once reserved exclusively for converts). While emphasizing tradition, the Holocaust, and an-tisemitism may help imbue a strong Jewish identity, alone they are not going to be enough to encourage Jewish Millennials to partic-ipate regularly in synagogue prayer services or to perform *mitzvot*. Trying to get Millennials to adopt a theology that includes com-mandedness is unlikely to succeed as well. Our communal goal thus needs to be to help each Millennial answer the question, "Why be

---

[271] This has serious theological implications as it relates to the traditional concepts of "Chosen People" and "Promised Land." After all, if there is no interactive God, then God couldn't designate certain people as "chosen" or certain land as "promised."

[272] God as all-powerful.

[273] God as all-knowing.

[274] "Jewish Americans in 2020," 70.

[275] "Jewish Americans in 2020," 71.

[276] Elyse Winick, "We Are All Jews by Choice." *YouTube*. Uploaded by Jewish Women's Archive, Sep. 10, 2020. www.youtube.com/watch?v=nveMIy1Fj14.

Jewish?" for themselves, encouraging them to find personal meaning in Jewish spiritual practices and the various *mitzvot*.

The High Holidays Problem

The High Holidays of Rosh Hashanah and Yom Kippur have a significant amount of special liturgy used exclusively for the associated prayer services, and much of it contains traditional, patriarchal, "God is judging our behavior" language. For example, a central prayer offered on the High Holidays is the *Unetaneh Tokef* which includes the following language:

> The great shofar is sounded, A still small voice is heard.
> The angels are dismayed, They are seized by fear and trembling
> As they proclaim: Behold the Day of Judgment!
> For all the hosts of heaven are brought for judgment.
> They shall not be guiltless in Your eyes
> And all creatures shall parade before You as a troop.
> As a shepherd herds his flock, Causing his sheep to pass beneath his staff,
> So do You cause to pass, count, and record, Visiting the souls of all living,
> Decreeing the length of their days, Inscribing their judgment.
> On Rosh Hashanah it is inscribed, And on Yom Kippur it is sealed.[277]

---

[277] Reuven Hammer, "Unetanah Tokef." My Jewish Learning. www.myjewishlearning.com/article/unetanah-tokef.

Behold the Day of Judgment! God is watching you to see if you've been naughty or nice, and whether you're going to be inscribed into the Book of Life or the Book of Death because of your behavior! Repent!

If, like most Millennials, you don't believe in an interactive God, then you certainly don't believe that God is judging you or deciding who will live and who will die each year. If the only time you show up for prayer services all year is on the High Holidays, without appropriate framing you'd be forgiven for thinking that Jews believe some interesting (dare I say dangerous?) things! And frankly, our day-to-day liturgy isn't much better.

There's a story about the Chassidic master, Reb Levi Yitzchak of Berditchev, that goes something like this:

> In the town of Berditchev, the home of the great Hassidic master, Reb Levi Yitzhak, there was a self-proclaimed, self-assured atheist, who would take great pleasure in publicly denying the existence of God. One day Reb Levi Yitzhak of Berditchev approached this man and said, "You know what, I don't believe in the same God that you don't believe in."[278]

While this approach might work when provided with the opportunity to engage with people individually, it's harder to execute with large groups, such as those who attend services exclusively on the High Holidays (although some rabbis have boldly tried).[279] But my impression is that the average congregant doesn't know that their clergy likely also doesn't believe in the God they themselves don't believe in. Our traditional liturgy can be alienating and doesn't align with most Millennials theologically, and requiring prayer service

---

[278] Marc Soloway, "The God I Don't Believe In." Berdichev.org, 2010. www.berdichev.org/the_god_i_dont_believe.html.
[279] Rabbi Michael Knopf's 2015 Yom Kippur eve sermon is a great example: https://mikeknopf.wordpress.com/2015/09/24/mastering-the-service-of-the-heart-kol-nidrei-57762015.

participants to say words they don't believe is challenging for Millennials who crave authenticity.

Authenticity

For Millennials, authenticity is key. To be authentic means to be "true to one's own personality, spirit, or character."[280] Google "Millennials and authenticity" and you'll find countless articles and studies emphasizing this desire.[281] When it comes to authenticity and Jewish prayer, expecting Millennials to pray in a language they don't speak or understand is a hard sell. Even worse would be having them pray in a language they do speak if the words they're saying don't align with their beliefs. English translations of Hebrew prayers often are problematic because, as Rabbi Marcia Prager writes in her book *The Path of Blessing*, "there are few English words to fully convey what the Hebrew expresses."[282]

I think Hebrew prayer is a blessing in this regard, as it can be mantra-esque. Those who aren't fluent Hebrew speakers don't have to think about what the words actually mean and can get lost in the music and chanting. With many Jews raised in the Conservative Movement now affiliating with Reform Movement congregations,[283] I think self-consciousness about the content of prayers when prayed in English is a primary (if unacknowledged) reason the Reform Movement has moved away from its classical roots and embraced praying in Hebrew.

Israelis, as native Hebrew speakers, obviously have a harder time with this concept, as they can't simply get lost in syllables when

---

[280] https://www.merriam-webster.com/dictionary/authentic.

[281] For example:Karl Moore, "Authenticity: The Way To The Millennial's Heart." *Forbes*, Aug. 14, 2014. www.forbes.com/sites/karlmoore/2014/08/14/authenticity-the-way-to-the-millennials-heart.

[282] Marcia Prager, *The Path of Blessing* (Jewish Lights, 2003), 26.

[283] Jacob Ausubel et al., "Denominational switching among U.S. Jews: Reform Judaism has gained, Conservative Judaism has lost." Pew Research Center, June 22, 2021. www.pewresearch.org/fact-tank/2021/06/22/denominational-switching-among-u-s-jews-reform-judaism-has-gained-conservative-judaism-has-lost.

they understand the words they're saying. I would posit this is a contributing factor to why there's a much larger group of Israelis who'll happily call themselves "secular" rather than embrace a liberal expression of Judaism. They can't tune out the meaning of the words they're saying the way non-Hebrew-speaking North American Jews can.

Some deal with this challenge by ascribing new, personal meanings to the traditional Hebrew words. For example, Jewish communal thought leader Dan Libenson has spoken about how Hebrew blessings often take on new meanings rather than their literal translations in the minds of those offering them. For example, he thinks that most people who offer a blessing at the Torah, known as an *aliyah*, think that what they're saying is, "Okay, it's time to bless the Torah now!" In reality, the blessing's literal translation includes references to God choosing the Jewish people from among the nations and giving them the Torah.[284]

Asking Millennials to come to services to pray in a language they don't understand and often can't read makes them self-conscious. Younger Jews are much more likely than their elders to say that a lack of knowledge about how to participate keeps them away from Jewish religious services,[285] and no one wants to feel left out or othered! Praying to a version of a God they don't believe in feels inauthentic. But for the sense of familial (as opposed to Divine) obligation and guilt, many of those who attend on the High Holidays would likely stand up and walk out if they could.

---

[284] Dan Libenson and Lex Rofeberg, "B-Mitzvah Revolutions." *Judaism Unbound*, Episode 85, Sep. 29, 2017. www.judaismunbound.com/podcast/2017/9/1/judaism-unbound-episode-85-b-mitzvah-revolutions-isa-aron.

[285] "Jewish Practices and Customs." Pew Research Center, May 11, 2021. www.pewforum.org/2021/05/11/jewish-practices-and-customs.

A Contemporary Millennial Theology

The Biblical and liturgical portrayals of God are constructs that overwhelmingly do not resonate with Millennials. But before you label me a heretic, it's important to remember that there is no shortage of communally accepted Jewish theologies.[286] Rabbi Elliot Dorff, a Jewish legal luminary, has written that within the Conservative Movement alone there are at least 4 acceptable theological positions on Revelation (the receiving of the Torah).[287] So, embracing new theologies is a very Jewish thing to do! (So is hating on those who have embraced new theologies.)[288] So what is a contemporary Jewish theology that will resonate with Millennials?

For many Millennials, the theology (or "God concept") that seems to resonate most is acknowledging that there is an interconnecting energy source that permeates our world and is beyond our comprehension. This energy source doesn't have any sort of consciousness. It is not inherently male. It doesn't have active control over our lives in any way. And it never before, nor does it now, engage with human beings in conversation. But it links us all together as individual parts of a greater whole.

Have you ever called someone on the phone, and the first thing they say to you is, "Wow! Your ears must have been burning! I was just talking about you!" The way it often presents for me is I mention the name of someone to my wife who I haven't spoken to in 6 months, and within 5 minutes I get a call or text from them. For some, this might be viewed as a simple coincidence. But when everything and everyone is interconnected, it isn't surprising we somehow know on a subconscious level when others are thinking about us.

---

[286] In their book *Finding God* (Union of American Hebrew Congregations, 1986), Rifat Sonsino and Daniel B. Syme share 10 different Jewish theologies!

[287] Elliot Dorff, *Conservative Judaism* (Youth Commission, United Synagogue of America, 1977), 98-99.

[288] Dutch Jewish philosopher Baruch Spinoza, exiled by Amsterdam's Portuguese Jews in 1656 for heresy, comes to mind!

Admittedly this God concept isn't uniquely Jewish in and of itself.[289] But just because a theology isn't uniquely Jewish doesn't make it less Jewish—especially if it's a theology held by a significant number of Jewish people (and happens to be rooted in Jewish philosophy and text). The "interconnecting energy source" theology also comfortably exists in concert with our current scientific understanding of the universe, eliminating concerns of faith being incongruent with science. Since authenticity is essential, Millennials are unwilling to divorce faith from observed reality. If a theology doesn't align with the scientific understanding of the world, the scientific understanding will win every time. So a contemporary Jewish theology needs to be one that is enmeshed with science.[290]

If there is indeed some sort of interconnecting energy source that permeates the world that is "God," how can we best understand why our ancestors decided to offer animal sacrifices to it? Or to pray to it? In trying to describe the indescribable, our ancestors ascribed human characteristics to it.

In one of the early stories in the Torah, we find Noah surviving the flood with his family. Immediately upon disembarking from the ark, they offer burnt animal sacrifices to God, who reportedly found the odor pleasing.[291] Does God really have a nose with which to enjoy the smells of BBQ? I don't know about you, but I love the smell of BBQ. While I've been a vegetarian for almost two decades, I can't help but admit that when I walk by a BBQ restaurant and smell the

---

[289] For a fantastic video parodying Millennial theology, see: "The Church for People Who Are 'Spiritual, But Not Religious.'" *YouTube*. Uploaded by CollegeHumor, Feb. 23, 2016. www.youtube.com/watch?v=Z78_rAg4Ldg

[290] The Dalai Lama taught the same about Buddhism: Tenzin Gyatso, "Our Faith in Science." The Office of His Holiness The Dalai Lama, Dec. 1, 2005. www.dalailama.com/news/2005/our-faith-in-science. There is now a Jewish nonprofit, Sinai and Synapses, focused on bridging the religious and scientific worlds: www.sinaiandsynapses.org.

[291] Genesis 8:20-21. Where did the animals for Noah to sacrifice come from? After all, "The animals, the animals, they came on by twosies, twosies" right? If so, wouldn't sacrificing any of them doom the survival of the species? Fear not! The Torah states (Genesis 7:2-3) that Noah brought on additional "pure" animals and birds, to be sacrificed to God after the flood.

smells, I start to salivate. The large number of BBQ pit-master shows on Netflix indicate I'm not alone in this. So, I'm not surprised that my ancestors, who enjoyed the smell of BBQ, would also assume that God enjoyed the smell of BBQ. But do I believe in a God who has a nose and appreciates the way things smell? No. Channeling my inner Reb Levi Yitzhak of Berditchev: I also don't believe in the God that you don't believe in!

Millennial Prayer

Those who are in the business of facilitating Jewish prayer experiences are in a tough spot. If their prayer services are primarily in Hebrew, many Millennials will feel self-conscious about not knowing the language and won't want to participate (especially if it's a fast "*davening*" style where even if they can parse Hebrew words they won't be able to keep up with the pace of the service). If the prayer services are primarily in English, many Millennials won't want to participate due to it feeling inauthentic, as the words they're saying generally don't align with their theological beliefs. Given these realities, what are those who are in the business of crafting Jewish prayer experiences to do?

Rabbi Arthur Green writes in *Radical Judaism* that, "[w]e need to build bridges that will allow contemporary seekers to overcome these problems of language...."[292] I'd humbly suggest Step 1 in building such a bridge is to get rid of the English word "God." It conjures a specific image for many of an old man in the sky with a beard who judges you. There are scores of Hebrew names for God—roughly 70 in the Bible and at least 90 more in rabbinic literature, not to mention those embraced by the Jewish mystics.[293] We should not feel bound by a particular English word and can be much more creative

---

[292] Arthur Green, *Radical Judaism* (Yale University Press, 2010), 73.
[293] Ismar Schorsch, "Behind God's Names." The Jewish Theological Seminary, Nov. 20, 1993. www.jtsa.edu/torah/behind-gods-names.

about using names that better speak to contemporary theologies. Whether "Divine," "Source of Life and Love," "*HaMakom*," or a slew of others, there are ways to combat the negative associated imagery. Using masculine pronouns for God and masculine names such as "Lord" should be avoided.[294] Contemporary language should be used whenever possible. The often used at funerals, "He maketh me lie down in green pastures" from Psalm 23 is right out! If I could, I'd maketh it such that the word "maketh" is never used in a Jewish setting ever again![295]

Additionally, the opportunity exists to use non-literal English translations that are inspired by our tradition and that will better resonate with Millennials. For example, instead of translating the traditional blessing construct of *Baruch Atah Adonai Eloheinu Melech HaOlam Asher Kid'shanu B'Mitzvotav V'Tzivanu…* as "Praised are you, Adonai our God, King of the Universe, who has hallowed us by your commandments and commanded us to…", we can use an interpretive translation more palatable to Millennials, such as: "We Acknowledge the Unity of All, and express gratitude for the opportunity to connect by…"

"The Unity of All"

We found that using the name/phrase "The Unity of All" worked equally well for those who held a more traditional belief in God as well as for those with different theologies (and even for avowed atheists). For believers, the language acknowledges the oneness of God and is informed by the Kabbalistic notion of *Ein Sof*—there is

---

[294] For a great article on this topic, see: Michael Knopf, "What Is in a Name, the Name of God?" *Haaretz*, June 3, 2012. www.haaretz.com/jewish/2012-06-03/ty-article/what-is-in-a-name-the-name-of-god/0000017f-f008-d497-a1ff-f28842a20000.

[295] I have a number of colleagues who tell me they believe their congregants find comfort in Psalm 23's Old English style translation in particular, as it's how they've always heard it. I understand their point. The problem is that it makes Judaism seem antiquated rather than relevant in an era where perceived relevance is key to our thriving, and it also makes us sound like 18th-century Christians.

no end—that God is everything and everything is God. For non-believers, the language contains the humanistic ethos of all people being interconnected in this world and responsible for one another as humans. It certainly aligns well with the "interconnecting energy source" theology favored by Millennials.

"The Opportunity to Connect"

While the word *mitzvah* literally means "commandment," it's taught in Chassidic circles that the root of the word *mitzvah* is *tzavta*—connection. Thus, *mitzvot* can be thought of as connection opportunities as opposed to commandments. For believers, the *mitzvot* are obligatory and provide an opportunity to deepen our relationship with and understanding of God. For non-believers, fulfilling *mitzvot* provides the opportunity to connect with the Jewish tradition, with community, etc.

Even with these kinds of modifications to English translations, for many Millennials the words themselves, regardless of the language, are a problem and get in the way of their ability to connect spiritually in a Jewish way. Admittedly a piece of this is many don't understand that much of the traditional liturgy is comprised of poetry that uses imagery and symbols to evoke emotion that will trigger self-reflection and growth, and that the words being offered need not be understood literally. However, when words get in the way we need to be open to getting rid of the words and create opportunities to connect spiritually in a Jewish way that avoids words at all.

Speechless Shabbat

If many Millennials don't know enough to participate in synagogue services and if the words often get in the way, what would it look like to create a Friday night Shabbat prayer service devoid of words that would simultaneously help Millennials feel more comfortable in traditional synagogue services?

Keen on creating that service, we piloted a concept at The Well called "Speechless Shabbat." Embracing the traditional arc of a Friday night service, we crafted brief thematically aligned meditations and intention statements, which we printed on a single sheet of cardstock for each participant, providing a "prayer page" rather than a "prayer book." During the prayer experience, each of these meditations was accompanied by a *niggun*—a wordless, repetitive melody—facilitated by a small group of instrumentalists and vocalists.

Embracing music is essential when crafting spiritual experiences for Millennials. As Rabbi Abraham Joshua Heschel wrote:

> "The only language that seems to be compatible with the wonder and mystery of being is the language of music. Music is more than just expressiveness. It is rather a reaching out toward a realm that lies beyond the reach of verbal propositions. Verbal expression is in danger of being taken literally and of serving as a substitute for insight. Words become slogan, slogans become idols. But music is a refutation of human finality. Music is an antidote to higher idolatry."[296]

Or, as put simply by Rabbi Naomi Levy: "[M]usic is prayer."[297]

Attendees silently read and reflected on a meditation inspired by part of the traditional Friday evening service while singing a wordless melody repeatedly using "lai lai lai," "nai nai nai," or "dai dai dai." We strategically chose melodies often paired with traditional Friday night liturgy. For example, for the *Shema*, a prayer which focuses on the Oneness of the Divine, our intention read as follows:

---

[296] Abraham J. Heschel, *The Insecurity of Freedom* (Farrar, Straus and Giroux, 1966), 245.
[297] Naomi Levy, *Einstein and the Rabbi* (Flatiron, 2018), 62.

> In a world constantly sub-sectioned and divided,
> it's sometimes hard to remember that we're all in-
> terconnected. That there is a Unity of All. Bring to
> your mind someone who is the opposite of you—be
> it politically, geographically, religiously, etc.—and
> focus on our shared humanity, and shared destiny.

The melody we then sang repeatedly during that part of the prayer experience was composed by Israeli musician Tzvika Pik (of blessed memory) for the Shema and is a melody used in many synagogues around the world during their services.[298] This was an intention-al choice, as we were familiarizing our participants with the music they might find in a synagogue prayer service while helping them internalize the themes of those particular prayers. In so doing, we hoped to provide for a meaningful spiritual experience in the moment while simultaneously making synagogue sanctuaries just a bit more familiar and less anxiety-inducing the next time they found themselves inside one.

Interfaithless Marriage

We can't really have a chapter that focuses on Millennial theology without spending at least a little bit of time discussing interfaith marriage. Much ink in the Jewish world has been devoted to the "problem" of interfaith marriages. For many years, the communal response was to combat this perceived assimilation. When the Council of Jewish Federations' ("CJF")[299] 1990 National Jewish Population Study was released, people were shocked to learn that more than 50% of Jews were marrying gentile partners.[300] In 1991,

---

[298] You can find and purchase the sheet music here: https://freshsheetmusic.com/tzvika-pik-sh-ma-hear-66290.
[299] Now known as the Jewish Federations of North America or JFNA.
[300] Barry A. Kosmin et al., "Highlights of the CJF 1990 National Jewish Population Survey." The Council of Jewish Federations, 1991. www.jewishdatabank.org/content/upload/bjdb/

CJF held a daylong symposium at their general assembly focused on "Intermarriage and Jewish Continuity."[301] With time and despite communal intervention efforts, the trend has intensified. According to recent data, we know that of Jews who married between 2010 and 2020, 72% of non-Orthodox Jews married someone who doesn't happen to be Jewish.[302] Let's not forget that roughly half of Jewish Millennials today are the products of an interfaith marriage who intermarry themselves at a clip of 82%.[303] As a result, while there are still some who are concerned with preventing these marriages from happening in the first place, much of the communal agenda has shifted to how best to welcome these families into Jewish life and community, viewing an interfaith marriage as welcoming someone new as opposed to treating the Jew who married a gentile as someone who has chosen to leave the community, having hurt it by "doing Hitler's job for him."[304]

Admittedly this has caused some interesting challenges for traditional Jewish institutions. For example, should Hebrew Free Loan societies, which offer interest-free loans to Jews, make dollars available to non-Jewish spouses, or for the non-Jewish widow(er)s of Jews?[305] How can Jewish Federations raise dollars in good faith from interfaith couples and then make allocations to Orthodox schools

---

Highlights_of_the_CJF_1990_National_Jewish_Population_Survey_Summary_Report_ v3.pdf, 14.

[301] "Symposium on Intermarriage and Jewish Continuity." Council of Jewish Federations. Volume 1. Nov. 20, 1991. www.bjpa.org/content/upload/bjpa/symp/SYMPOSIUM%20 ON%20INTERMARRIAGE%20&%20JEWISH%20CONTINUITY%20VOL%20I%201991. pdf.

[302] "Jewish Americans in 2020." Pew Research Center, May 11, 2021. www.pewresearch.org/ religion/wp-content/uploads/sites/7/2021/05/PF_05.11.21_Jewish.Americans.pdf, 93.

[303] "Jewish Americans in 2020," 98.

[304] Matt Lebovic, "When American Jews described their own intermarriage as a 'Second Holocaust.'" *The Times of Israel*, July 12, 2019. www.timesofisrael.com/when-american-jews-described-their-own-intermarriage-as-a-second-holocaust.

[305] There are some who argue that the term "non-Jewish" should be abandoned from the Jewish lexicon: David Evan Markus, "'Say No to Non!'— Let's Ban the Phrase 'Non-Jew.'" My Jewish Learning, Apr. 26, 2018. www.myjewishlearning.com/2018/04/26/say-no-to-non-lets-ban-the-phrase-non-jew.

where the marriages of those couples are being denigrated? How should we be thinking about the long-term implications when it comes to Israel's Law of Return[306] and who counts as Jewish there? The answers aren't easy.

Despite a (slim) majority of the Conservative Movement's congregants wanting its rabbis to officiate at interfaith weddings,[307] as of this writing the Rabbinical Assembly (the Conservative Movement's rabbinic union) doesn't permit them to do so.[308] Yet most of the movement's congregations welcome interfaith couples to join as members and the United Synagogue of Conservative Judaism has a designated webpage and programs seeking to support congregations in welcoming interfaith couples.[309] Being turned away by rabbis when it's time to celebrate their marriage and then hoping they'll join synagogue communities where they experienced rejection isn't an ideal strategy,[310] and it's no wonder that of the interfaith couples who do affiliate with synagogues, most are choosing Reform congregations. I believe there are two additional reasons for this. First, the Reform Movement recognized patrilineal descent in 1983[311]—that is, so long as you have one Jewish parent and are living a committed Jewish life, you're deemed Jewish in the Reform Movement, while in the Conservative and Orthodox movements you're only

---

[306] Some Israeli politicians are trying to amend the law to make immigration more restrictive: Arno Rosenfeld, "'Not a theocracy': Proposed change to Israel's Law of Return sparks concern." *Forward*, Nov. 14, 2022. www.forward.com/fast-forward/524761/israel-law-of-return-changes-conservative-reform-orthodox.

[307] "Jewish Americans in 2020," 99.

[308] Ari Feldman, "With Intermarriage Endorsement, Rabbi Hopes To Start 'Grass Roots' Movement." *Forward*, Dec. 19, 2018. www.forward.com/news/416230/with-intermarriage-endorsement-rabbi-hopes-to-start-grass-roots-movement.

[309] "Interfaith Inclusion." United Synagogue of Conservative Judaism. www.uscj.org/leadership/interfaith-inclusion.

[310] "No matter how nicely you say it, declining to perform someone's wedding implies a cruel rejection." Jeremy Kalmanofsky, "Why I Will Not Simply Accept Intermarriage." *Forward*, Mar. 8, 2015.www.forward.com/opinion/216123/why-i-will-not-simply-accept-intermarriage.

[311] "The Status of Children of Mixed Marriages." Central Conference of American Rabbis, Mar. 15, 1983.
www.jewishvirtuallibrary.org/reform-movement-s-resolution-on-patrilineal-descent-march-1983.

considered Jewish if your mother is Jewish.[312] Second, many more Reform Jews than Conservative Jews intermarry.[313] Also troubling are the inevitable micro-aggressions that many of these couples are met with across denominations, as it's still normative to hear people say to the parents of young children things like, "Just wait until he grows up and finds a nice Jewish girl to marry!" Aside from being heteronormative, this also assumes the parent they're talking to isn't part of an interfaith couple or isn't the product of an interfaith marriage themselves. Recent research conducted by 18Doors found that more than 50% of interfaith couples not actively participating in Jewish life said they would like to, with organizational CEO Jodi Bromberg writing that "they reported that they had not found a Jewish community that felt comfortable for them or inclusive of interfaith families."[314]

For those concerned about Jewish continuity, the math argues for viewing interfaith marriages as a Jewish communal growth opportunity. Let's say there are 10 Jewish people. Four of them marry Jews, and six of them marry non-Jews. The four Jews marrying other Jews result in two Jewish-Jewish family units (that is, the Jews marry each other, and four Jews marrying one another becomes two couples). The six Jews marrying non-Jews result in six interfaith family units. A majority of interfaith families are raising their children Jewish,[315] and the percentage is actively rising.[316] For simple math's sake, let's say that half of the six interfaith family units choose to not have a Jewish home or raise their children Jewish. In such a scenario, you'd still have three interfaith families raising Jewish children—more

---

[312] All 3 denominations also have conversion processes for those who elect to become Jewish.
[313] "Jewish Americans in 2020," 98.
[314] Jodi Bromberg, "Interfaith Families." *Warm and Welcoming*, edited by Warren Hoffman and Miriam Steinberg-Egeth (Rowman & Littlefield, 2021), 27.
[315] Ben Sales, "Most children of intermarriage are being raised Jewish." *The Jerusalem Post*, May 14, 2021. www.jpost.com/diaspora/most-children-of-intermarriage-are-being-raised-jewish-668154.
[316] "Jewish Americans in 2020," 44.

than the two Jewish-Jewish families! That said, research does show different outcomes as it relates to communal engagement, affiliation, Israel attachment and the like when comparing Jewish-Jewish and interfaith families, largely due to interfaith families raising their children as culturally rather than religiously Jewish.[317]

The term "interfaith" is therefore problematic itself because what it misses is that these marriages are often interfaith*less*. Very rarely have I come across an interfaith couple in which both partners are actively practicing their inherited faith tradition in a traditional manner. While there are certainly some couples who might be "interfaithful,"[318] the Jewish community generally has not been particularly welcoming to them. For example, even the comparatively inclusive Reform Movement has not historically permitted its rabbis to co-officiate weddings with clergy members of other faiths[319] and has insisted that the children of interfaith couples be raised exclusively Jewish to be counted as Jews.[320]

For the adherents of many faiths (including Judaism, Catholicism, etc.), religious dogma indicates that marrying within the faith is expected. If you're a traditionally observant Jew for example, the Talmud is explicit that you are prohibited from marrying a gentile.[321] Only 2% of married Orthodox-identifying Jews say they have a non-Jewish spouse.[322] But as we know, most Jewish Millennials are not traditionally observant or Orthodox, so marriage involving a Jew and a non-Jew generally includes at least one partner who is secular/cultural. In my experience, having worked with scores of couples

---

[317] "Jewish Americans in 2020," 40.

[318] Vivian Henoch, "Interfaithful Couple." *My Jewish Detroit*, Nov. 29, 2018. www.myjewishdetroit.org/2018/11/29/interfaithful-couple.

[319] "Ecumenical Wedding Ceremonies: Co-Officiation with Clergy of Other Faiths." Central Conference of American Rabbis, 1982. www.ccarnet.org/ccar-resolutions/ecumenical-wedding-ceremonies-co-officiation-with-clergy-of-other-faiths-1982.

[320] "Dual Religion Family." Central Conference of American Rabbis, 1995. www.ccarnet.org/responsa-topics/dual-religion-family.

[321] Babylonian Talmud, Avodah Zarah, Folio 36b.

[322] "Jewish Americans in 2020," 93.

leading up to and then officiating their weddings (a significant number of whom had partners with different religious backgrounds), even if the couple wants a rabbi to officiate or co-officiate their ceremony it was often courtesy of a desire to include Jewish wedding traditions such as smashing a glass at the end of the ceremony or to try and please one's parents or grandparents. It had nothing to do with God or "sanctifying" the marriage religiously.

Some like Rabbi Denise Handlarski have suggested a more appropriate term than interfaith would be "intercultural."[323] Personally, I've taken to referring to these couples as "interfaithless," or in a more positive framing as "mixed-heritage." 18Doors, the primary national Jewish nonprofit organization focused on engaging these couples in Jewish life, actually changed its name from "InterfaithFamily" due to many couples not identifying with the term "interfaith."[324] Millennial alienation from traditional Jewish liturgy and theology is even more present for mixed-heritage couples as the non-Jewish partner likely has no familiarity with Hebrew or Jewish prayer, and with the couple often living a largely secular life traditional prayer and its emphasis on God is unlikely to speak to them.

Being sensitive to the needs of these couples is key. Often the Jewish partner feels self-conscious and hesitant to approach a rabbi, concerned their love won't be celebrated due to generations of guilt and decades of proposed "interventions" by the organized Jewish community. The simple truth is that there are wonderful human beings in this world who don't happen to be Jewish who will make wonderful partners for our own Jewish children. The question thus isn't, "How do we prevent this from happening?" because it's inevitably going to happen in a free and open society (especially if you're not raising your children in a traditionally religious construct). Rather, our focus must be on how we make being part of Jewish com-

---

[323] Denise Handlarski, *The A-Z of Intermarriage* (New Jewish Press, 2020), 36.
[324] "Our Rebranding." 18Doors, 2020. www.18doors.org/rebranding.

munity so welcoming, joyous, meaningful, relevant, and substantive that these couples can't imagine not wanting to be actively part of it themselves and are excited about raising any future offspring within it as well. We've already seen shifts in communal attitude and accompanying inclusion efforts result in a significant increase in the number of mixed-heritage families choosing to raise their children Jewish.[325] As in all things Millennial engagement, relationships are key. Turning away, shaming, or simply "tolerating" mixed-heritage couples as opposed to embracing them is a missed opportunity to begin forming lasting relationships with them.

Israel

If Millennials don't believe in an interactive God, then they also don't believe in a God who chooses certain people over others or promises certain lands to them. The overwhelming majority of North American Jews, regardless of age/generation, don't believe that God gave the land that is now Israel to the Jewish people.[326] And we know that in many communities Israel has become a wedge issue.[327] Absent a belief in a Divinely promised land, how do Millennials understand and think about Israel?

We know that younger American Jews are less emotionally attached to Israel than older ones[328] and that fewer than half of those ages 18-49 view caring about Israel as essential to being Jewish.[329] Even with Birthright Israel taking hundreds of thousands of Millennials on free trips, the majority of American Jewish Millennials have never visited Israel,[330] and a significant percentage of them actually view the US as being too supportive of Israel.[331]

---

[325] "Jewish Americans in 2020," 44-45.
[326] Ibid., 155.
[327] Ibid., 156.
[328] Ibid., 139.
[329] Ibid., 141.
[330] Ibid., 138.
[331] Ibid., 144.

Whatever my concerns may be about Birthright Israel's marketing techniques, there's no doubt it has been a catalyst for many to begin building a meaningful personal relationship with Israel. Millennials (not Jewish ones specifically) think that Israel is the second most religious country in the world, between Saudi Arabia and Iran.[332] So one of the things that Birthright participants often find most eye opening is how one can be Jewish in Israel without having to be religious, as for the first time they see Judaism as a nationality and culture as opposed to a religion.[333] You're Jewish just walking down the street in Tel Aviv, or hanging out at the beach with Hebrew language and music surrounding you, the Star of David on your flag, etc. No synagogue attendance or traditional theology is required to feel Jewish in Israel!

I'd liken a Birthright trip experience to the initial courtship/infatuation phase of a relationship, in that the trips are designed to get you excited about and interested in Israel and to make you desire to be in relationship with it. And while it's a great first step, a Birthright trip alone is often not sufficient. If a relationship remains purely superficial—at the infatuation level—it's likely to fade with time. As discussed earlier, Millennials crave authenticity—not talking points. They want to get to know, see and experience the real Israel.

In my estimation, a major mistake the organized Jewish world has made when it comes to Millennials and Israel is leaning into an advocacy construct (often referred to as *hasbara*) as opposed to an educational one. One needs to be in a meaningful relationship with Israel and Israelis to be able to authentically advocate for the country. And the way a meaningful relationship is formed is for there to be deep learning about one another. Advocacy without education

---

[332] Noa Tishby, *Israel* (Free Press, 2022), 264. Citing: David Sable, "Defining What Israel Means." Consulate General of Israel in New York, Nov. 2019. www.vmlyr.com/sites/www/files/2020-11/Brand%20Israel%202019%20Deck%2011%2013%2019.pdf.
[333] Zvika Klein, "1/4 American Jewish millennials distance themselves from Israel to fit in." *The Jerusalem Post*, Apr. 25, 2022. www.jpost.com/diaspora/article-705059.

is simply surface level attraction—it's shallow. And when put to the test, superficial relationships crumble.

One of my favorite poems is called "Tourists" by prize-winning Israeli poet and author Yehuda Amichai (1924-2000). The second stanza has always resonated with me deeply:

> Once I sat on the steps by a gate at David's Tower,
> I placed my two heavy baskets at my side. A group
> of tourists was standing around their guide and I
> became their target marker. "You see that man with
> the baskets? Just right of his head there's an arch from
> the Roman period. Just right of his head." "But he's
> moving, he's moving!" I said to myself: redemption
> will come only if their guide tells them, "You see that
> arch from the Roman period? It's not important: but
> next to it, left and down a bit, there sits a man who's
> bought fruit and vegetables for his family."[334]

Amichai's message is that the people who live in Israel are real people, having real human experiences. Yes, see the sights and learn the history. Yes, be appreciative of the architecture and the ruins and the nostalgia. But don't forget that your average Israeli (including Arabs and other minority populations) is trying to make a living, have a safe place to sleep at night, and to feed and love their families.

One of the best partnerships we cultivated at The Well was with JDC Entwine—the American Jewish Joint Distribution Committee's young adult department. We partnered on a weeklong "Inside Israel" trip together, introducing participants to various civil society building projects the JDC was working on across Israel. The trip's participants learned that like any modern society, Israeli society has challenges, underserved populations, doesn't always make great de-

---

[334] Yehuda Amichai, "Tourists." *Israel: Voices from Within*. Trans. Glenda Abramson and Tudor Parfitt. (Third Place Publications, 2020), 108-109.

cisions when it comes to equitable resource allocation, and more. I'd liken this to seeing the person you've been infatuated with without makeup on for the first time, wearing grungy sweatpants and having a bad hair day. We love our committed romantic partners because of their flaws—not despite them. In the same vein, holding Israel up on a pedestal does nobody any favors in the long run. Israel is a real place full of real people and has real opportunities and challenges. Education is the key to a deep, lasting relationship. Advocacy alone is not.

Just as Millennials are unwilling to divorce faith from reason and require an aligned theology, so too Millennials can't divorce core American values such as democracy, support of the rule of law and equal justice for all, from what they expect of Israel. As Rabbi Daniel Gordis writes in his book *We Stand Divided*: "To American sensibilities, there is something deeply disturbing about the legal and cultural implications of a country being a specifically *Jewish* country."[335] As discussed in Chapter 1, the tension between the particular and universal is very real for Millennials. The balance (or lack thereof) between Jewish and democratic when it comes to Israel's state identity and Israeli government policy, particularly as it relates to where Palestinians and their needs fit into the region's geopolitical realities, makes many Millennials uncomfortable. Being in a real—not superficial—relationship with Israel is what will allow for American Jewish Millennials to embrace the country and its people and to not walk away from the relationship entirely from a sense of discomfort or disinterest.

---

[335] Daniel Gordis, *We Stand Divided* (Ecco, 2019), 169.

Core Takeaways

1. Our ancestors, prophets and rabbis didn't exclusively use the English word "God." Why should we? Consider eliminating the English word "God," along with any translations that refer to God using masculine pronouns and/or that include Old English.
2. Explore using interpretive translations of Hebrew prayers that, while rooted in tradition, are accessible to and embraceable by believers, non-believers, and non-Jewish significant others.
3. Acknowledge Millennial theology, recognize it as authentically Jewish, and broadcast that it is shared by many Jews—including rabbis!
4. Actively communicate—especially on the High Holidays—that much of the traditional liturgy is poetry, is meant to evoke emotions, and shouldn't be taken literally.
5. Experiment with putting traditional liturgy aside, getting rid of the words when they get in the way, and experiencing different ways of connecting spiritually as a community.
6. Embrace that a sizable and growing number of Jewish families include those who don't happen to be Jewish and be strategic about how best to welcome these folks in and have them feel included in all that Jewish communal life has to offer.
7. Adopt an educational posture toward Israel. It'll lead to a deeper relationship and, in turn, advocacy.

Discussion Questions

- How does our organization cater to the people who are more interested in talking to Goldberg than talking to God?
- Do our organization's liturgical selections, translations, and expressed theology align with the needs, desires and beliefs of those we're serving? If not, why not?
- How is our organization helping individuals answer the question, "Why be Jewish?" for themselves?
- If we haven't already, how can our organization move from a place of tolerating mixed-heritage couples to a place of embracing them?
- Does our organization approach Israel from a place of advocacy or from a place of education? What factors have led to this approach?

Conclusion

The day is short and the work is plentiful.
—Pirke Avot, 2:15

So, we've covered quite a bit in this book. From coffee dates to B-brands to fundraising techniques to theology and more. My hope is that you've come away feeling excited, challenged, and intrigued. As a Jewish community, we have so much to be proud of and we have much important work ahead of us. While The Well never set up a literal "liberal *tefillin* cart" near the *Kotel*, we did build Metro Detroit's inclusive Jewish community, education, and spirituality outreach initiative, focusing on the needs of Millennials with ripples felt well beyond.

I left my role with The Well in the spring of 2020, soon after the pandemic hit, to serve as the CEO of the Alper JCC in Miami (I signed my contract on March 3, 2020, a week before the world shut down). There, I had the opportunity not only to steer the organization through the early phases of the pandemic but also to pilot several of this book's Core Takeaways in a Legacy Organization setting.

In addition to successfully implementing and building upon The Well's fundraising campaign model, as highlighted in Chapter 6, we updated the Alper JCC's mission statement to reflect a commitment to human flourishing, making sure we used the word "inclusive," emphasized relevance, and included Jewish wisdom:

> Alper JCC Miami is a nonprofit organization com-
> mitted to human flourishing and cultivating a South
> Miami-Dade Jewish community that is inclusive, in-

spiring and relevant. To that end, we provide high quality social, cultural, educational, physical and recreational opportunities for individuals ages 6 weeks through the golden years. We boast a nurturing early childhood development center, a spirited summer camp, a non-judgmental fitness center, top notch tennis and swimming offerings, and a deep commitment to the arts. Our community-building efforts are driven by the Jewish teaching that every human being has infinite worth.

We embraced partnerships by inviting the community's synagogues and other organizations to participate in a virtual community-wide *Tashlich*[336] ceremony (this was a signature program we'd cultivated at The Well, so there was a blueprint in existence). Together we crafted a ceremony, and for weeks leading up to the gathering provided the opportunity for people to write down their perceived shortcomings on slips of hydro-degradable paper. As part of the ceremony, those slips of paper were then dropped into Biscayne Bay from an aerial drone. A new take on an ancient tradition!

We also experimented with for-profit models that would allow us to accomplish Jewish educational goals, such as contracting with a goat yoga company to offer "ScapeGoat Yoga" during the High Holidays,[337] and "Chad Gadyoga" in the lead-up to Passover.[338] Goat yoga is a thing and is incredibly popular![339] The sessions quickly sold

---

[336] During the High Holiday season, there's a ritual known as *Tashlich* where we cast away our perceived shortcomings (I hate the word "sins"), usually in the form of breadcrumbs tossed into a natural flowing body of water.

[337] On Yom Kippur afternoon, the *Avodah* service is traditionally recited, which recalls the High Priest symbolically placing the sins of the people onto a goat and sending it out into the wilderness. It's where the concept of a "scapegoat" comes from! (Found in Leviticus 16:22-23).

[338] One of the popular drinking songs found at the end of the Passover Seder is "*Chad Gadya*"— "just one kid" (kid=baby goat).

[339] AJ Willingham, "'Goat yoga' is a thing - and hundreds are lining up for it." *CNN*, Jan 12, 2017. www.cnn.com/2017/01/12/health/goat-yoga-oregon-trnd.

out, and the JCC made money. At each of these gatherings we were able to teach about the upcoming Jewish holiday and give folks the chance to do a yoga practice with goats (most of whom were well behaved) jumping on their backs. These gatherings made the news,[340] are now repeated annually at the Alper JCC, and with our guidance have been replicated in other communities as well.

We wove Shared Interest Groups together, focusing on young family play groups in certain geographic areas. Inspired by the PJ Library Parent Ambassador program,[341] we hired an ambassador for 10 hours a week whose job it was to coffee date and then link families together with one another, helping them find new best friends to do Jewish and life with. Courtesy of the relationships cultivated, a significant number of those families ended up sending their kids— together—to our JCC summer camp for the first time.

The past two years, I had the privilege of serving as one of the rabbis of a large Conservative synagogue in Metro Detroit, where we began implementing several of this book's Core Takeaways. Change is a process and takes time. Don't feel like you must implement the strategies offered throughout this book overnight. But as Rabbi Tarfon teaches in Pirke Avot 2:15—"The day is short and the work is plentiful." My hope is that the Jewish organizational world will embrace this book's Core Takeaways, and that the Discussion Questions will serve as meaningful conversation starters for our community's organizational leaders and stakeholders.

A Final Thought

Whenever I'm having a moment of self-doubt or concern about the future of the Jewish people and our institutions, I come back to

---

[340] Bobby Dyer, "Goat Yoga at the Alper JCC Educates and Entertains." *Community Rec Magazine*, Oct. 8, 2020. www.communityrecmag.com/goat-yoga-alper-jcc-educates-entertains.
[341] To learn more about the PJ Library Ambassador program, see: Deborah Moon, "Parent ambassadors connect PJ Library families." Jewish Federation of Greater Portland, Sep. 14, 2021. www.jewishportland.org/jewishreview/jr-stories/pj-library-ambassadors.

Rabbi Irwin Kula's teaching that religion is meant to be a toolbox in the service of human flourishing.[342] That is, that the purpose of religion—any religion—is to help human beings flourish. Rabbi Kula's understanding of "flourishing" mirrors the peak of Maslow's hierarchy of needs, which is "self-actualization," and I tend to use the terms interchangeably. Self-actualization in the Maslowian sense refers to the realization of a person's potential; seeking personal growth and peak experiences, allowing a person to become the most they can be.[343]

Judaism can help us self-actualize, inviting us into lives of meaning, purpose, love, and community. Being part of Jewish community is powerful and should nourish our lives holistically. And if Millennials don't find that to be the case, they will simply walk away.

Segmentation between the definably Jewish and not Jewish parts of oneself isn't an option. Our goal should be for people to examine their Jewish ties and say, "While I may not have always recognized or appreciated it, I attribute who I am and how I walk in this world, both as a Jew and as a human being, to being part of the Jewish community. I can't imagine not wanting to be actively part of this community for the rest of my life, and to share it with anyone who's interested."

Our rallying cry as a community, simply put, needs to be:

"Being actively part of Jewish community will help you flourish—helping you be the best version of yourself you can be."

That is our value proposition. Nothing less.

---

[342] Nicha Ratana and Saul Kaplan, "This Is Why Religion Is Just a Technology." *TIME*, July 25, 2014. www.time.com/3032104/religion-technology-irwin-kula.
[343] Saul Mcleod, "Maslow's Hierarchy Of Needs Theory." *Simply Psychology*, Mar. 2, 2023. www.simplypsychology.org/maslow.html.

TL;DR
(Millennial-speak for "Here's a quick summary of the entire book")

1. Relationships are everything.
2. Meet Millennials where they're at on their journeys, without judgment.
3. Shabbat Dinner is awesome.
4. Help people find friends to do Jewish and life with.
5. Embrace inclusion.
6. Build with, not for.
7. Facilitate partnerships.
8. Get out of your building.
9. Educate toward philanthropy.
10. Strategically leverage donations.
11. Infuse Jewish wisdom and emphasize its relevance.
12. Reimagine Jewish spirituality.
13. Relationships are everything.

Afterword
by Zack Bodner

When my three children were young, my wife and I took them to Disneyland. We did it all: We ate cotton candy, took selfies with Mickey and Minnie, and went on all the rides. One of my kids may have been a bit too young for the Matterhorn and Space Mountain rides, so I'm not claiming any "parent of the year" awards, but they were all old enough to go on the It's A Small World ride. And that's where I had my epiphany.

Now, if you've never been on that ride, here's how it goes: You sit on benches in a wide, flat-bottomed boat, and as the boat enters a dark tunnel, slowly bumping from side to side along a snaking, narrow river, the song "It's a Small World" begins to play on an interminable loop. When the lights come up, you see dioramas on both sides that depict different countries around the world—rolling hills with small houses and trees, (mechanized) people and animals, all rocking back and forth singing the same song. Each country and culture are depicted tastefully, if not traditionally, with Japanese in kimonos, Indians in saris, Arabs in robes, etc. (Israel is not represented, by the way, though there is one Jewish couple dressed in Orthodox clothing under a chuppah.)

As we were floating along the river, suddenly the ride stopped. We sat there for a while not moving, wondering what was happening, and finally a voice announced over the speakers that there was some technical difficulty, and we would have to wait until it was fixed. That wait turned into two hours! And after hearing that song play over and over for two hours, with my kids growing more and more impatient, it was enough to make me homicidal. Yet somehow, I had a moment of clarity.

I thought to myself: When my kids are old enough to go out on their own, I hope they explore the world, experience other exotic places and incredible people, fall in love with different food, music, art, and cultures. BUT I want them to know who they are—I want them to know that they are Jews, and I want them to return to their tradition because they love their Jewishness.

At that moment, I realized that my task as their father is to help them fall in love with their Jewishness. I also realized that as a community leader, it's my job to help my community fall in love with their Jewishness as well. So, I have spent the last 18 years as a parent and 25 years as a professional Jew, making that mission my top priority.

One of the most important lessons I've learned along the way is what brings meaning to Jewish life is the DOING. It's not enough to just BE Jewish. It's not enough to have Jewish relatives or have a DNA test that shows you are 98% Ashkenazi and then do nothing about it. To be sure, if you do nothing you're still Jewish, of course— we'll still claim you as part of the family—but not doing anything is a missed opportunity. You must act. You must engage. You must DO Jewish for Jewish life to be fulfilling.

Doing Jewish can give your life immeasurable meaning. It can help you find a sense of belonging to a community. It can give you a deeper connection to a people that has preexisted you for thousands of years and will outlast you for many more. Its values can guide you. Its rituals and holidays can help you mark time and create sacred moments. It can enrich your life beyond words.

But it's not always so easy to do Jewish. Sometimes it can be intimidating or inaccessible. Sometimes it can feel archaic and anachronistic. Sometimes we can just be too busy or have other priorities, so we choose not to.

That's why it is incumbent upon those of us responsible for passing the torch to the next generation (and frankly, who among us is NOT charged with that responsibility?) to create new ways to inspire them in the doing. This ever-evolving challenge requires creativity, passion, and tenacity. It requires exciting, innovative experimentation. It requires leaders who inspire the rest of us ... which brings me to this book.

How fortunate are we that Dan Horwitz has come along and written *Just Jewish* for just this moment?! Dan's passionate, articulate, and compelling call to action ought to be heeded by anyone who cares about the future of Jewish life. If you want to share the beauty of our tradition with a Millennial in your life, if you want to make Jewish life meaningful, relevant, and joyful for the next generation, then you must respond with equal passion to Dan's heartfelt plea. You must reply, "*Hineini*! Here I am!"

After reading *Just Jewish*, I have so many takeaways that I plan to bring to my own JCC. For starters, it was refreshing to learn that we need to stop make everything free for Millennials, thinking that's what will finally bring them through our doors. I love this notion that Dan says, "We're creating mercenaries rather than loyal soldiers" by paying them to do Jewish. He reminds us that they're willing to pay for things they value, like Pelotons and avocado toast, so we just need to demonstrate a little Jewish value and they'll pay for it. Of course!

I also love the idea of "Empowerment-Centric Co-Creation." I watch my kids uploading their own videos onto social media as much as they want to watch others, so what took me so long to realize this? In fact, why limit this strategy just to Millennials? I think there are people of all ages and backgrounds who want to co-create their own experiences these days, so let's empower them to do so.

Dan's suggestion to use virtual spaces as recognition tools the way we have traditionally used brick-and-mortar spaces is brilliant.

For example, giving a personal shout-out to young adult donors on their Facebook wall since they can't yet afford the types of gifts that would put Larry David to shame is genius. It's one more play from Dan's playbook I plan to take back to my JCC.

Engaging next-gen Jews is a holy task—one that I share with you—and as we engage in this holy work, we need clear guidebooks and visionary guides to lead us along the path, to show us the way, and to motivate us to keep on going. Fortunately, we now have an exceptional new manual to add to our canon, as Dan has given us a gift with this book and has proven himself to be a trailblazer on this journey.

It's hard for me to predict what the future of Jewish life will look like, but I know this: our grandchildren will not do Jewish the way our grandparents did. If we want them to do Jewish at all, if we want them to appreciate the beauty in our world but still love who they are and where they came from, we need to take Dan's lessons to heart and implement his strategies now. The future of Jewish life just might depend on it.

Acknowledgments

*If your friend did you a small favor, let
it be in your eyes a big favor.*
—Avot D'Rabbi Natan, 41:11

There is no shortage of people to thank for helping me reach this *shehecheyanu* moment.

At the risk of leaving someone out by accident (my apologies in advance if you're that person!), I'm going to name some important names.

I am profoundly grateful to:

~ Lori Talsky, The Well's visionary and generous pilot donor, for taking a chance on me, for serving as a valued source of creative ideas and encouragement, and for making all of our work possible. The Metro Detroit Jewish community, the Jewish world, and I personally owe you a true debt of gratitude.

~ Rabbi Paul Yedwab, my mentor, teacher and friend, for giving me the opportunity of a lifetime to run and build, for constantly pushing me to think bigger and differently, and for always making himself available when I needed an ear. Thank you, Paul, for all you've done and continue to do on behalf of the Jewish people. And thank you for writing the Foreword to this book as well!

~ Temple Israel of Metropolitan Detroit, including the full clergy and staff team, lay leadership, and in particular past congregational presidents Julie August and Hilary King, for having the foresight and strength to embrace a disruptor as your own, even when we were working out the kinks. The Well simply wouldn't flow without your essential support.

~ Our major organizational funders over the years, including: The Farber Family Foundation, The Covenant Foundation (with particular gratitude to Harlene Appelman, of blessed memory), The Ravitz Foundation, The Max and Marjorie Fisher Foundation, The Mandell and Madeleine Berman Foundation, The Gilbert Family Foundation, and The Blumenstein Family Foundation. Thank you all for investing in vibrant Jewish life in Metro Detroit and beyond!

~ The organizations that invested in my professional development, including Moishe House and their Open Dor Project, Rabbi Sid Schwarz's Clergy Leadership Incubator and Kenissa Network, The Charles and Lynn Schusterman Family Philanthropies' ROI Community, and ELI Talks. I will forever be grateful to you all for helping me to grow in so many ways.

~ Those who helped to amplify The Well's work and impact, with particular thanks to Slingshot, eJewishPhilanthropy, *Judaism Unbound*, the *Detroit Jewish News*, the *Detroit Free Press*, the *Detroit News*, and the *Forward*.

~ Those I had the privilege of having as my professional teammates at The Well, who went above and beyond in service to our mission, and who became family: Avery Markel, Matt Weiner, Brandon Klein, Marisa Meyerson and Mimi Marcus.

~ The Well's board (aka "Bucket List") members during my tenure: Alyah Al-Azem, Adam Denenberg, Audrey Bloomberg, Connie Gaines, Danny Rosenberg, Dima Gutin, Gabe Neistein, Gabe Scharg, George Roberts, Ian Gross, Jacob Krause, Jessica Katz, Julie Bagley, Katie Wallace, Laura Feldman Weiner, Lauren Sterling, Lowell Weiss, Matthew Ross, Miriam Horwitz, Nicole Reich, Samantha Friedman, Sid Kaye, Steve Hurvitz, Tara Schonberger, and Zac Berlin. Co-creating with you all, and building The Well together brick by brick, was truly a privilege. Thanks for all the late-night meetings, for showing up for community, and for leading the charge.

~ The Well's senior advisory board: Bob Rubin, Brenda Rosenberg, David Gad-Harf, Kelly Sternberg, Ron Elkus and Steve Blum. Thank you all for facilitating strategic introductions, making yourselves available whenever I needed an ear, and for believing in our work!

~ The Well's Champion Challengers, dynamic brother duo Josh Kaplan and Darryl Kaplan, for your generosity, friendship, guidance, thought partnership, and outsized impact you had on The Well and our successes.

~ The Well's Champions, for turning the conventional notion that Millennials aren't willing to invest in Jewish community on its head: Aaron and Casey Rosenhaus, Adam and Lauren Blanck, Adam and Marla Jahnke, Adam and Hannah Kessler, Allen and Shana Weiss, Andrew Banooni, Ariella and Tzvi Raviv, Audrey Bloomberg and Tzvi Tanenbaum, Brett and Stephanie Mellin, Dana and Jon Miller, Daniel and Pauline Feldman, Daniel and Nicole Friedberg, Danielle and Matthew Newman, Danny and Jacqui Seidman, Danny Wiener, Dima and Tracy Gutin, Eddie and Elise Aronowitz, Evy Zwiebach and Alexa Shaw, George and Sarah Roberts, Hillary and Craig Glaser, Ian and Erin Gross, Jason and Nechama Lurie, Jonathan Schwartz and Stacy Trosell, Jordan and Lauren Acker, Jordan Zlotoff, Justin and Monique Jacobs, Kelly and Mike Sternberg, Kurt Liethen and Yuliya Malayev, Laura Feldman Weiner, Lowell and Colleen Weiss, Matt Cohn and Athena Akram, Matt and Jodie Ran, Matthew Ross, Max and Ksenia Milstein, Michael and Robin Berman, Michael and Shannon Benson, Nicole Reich, Rick and Connie Gaines, Roman Golshteyn, Sammi and Michael Shapiro, Sandy Nelson, Shimon and Jennie Levy, Steve and Tammy Hurvitz, Steven Davis and Jacob Krause, Tamara and Ben Friedman.

~ The Well's hundreds of co-creators and donors, and thousands of participants—our community. Thank you for building with us. For sharing coffee dates with us. For allowing us to be part of your Jewish journeys. For trusting us. And for investing your time, talent, and treasure in our community.

~ The Well's dozens of organizational partners, both local and national: thanks for being willing to share the sandbox with us, and for proving time and time again that when we work together, the total of what we build will always be greater than the sum of its individual parts.

~ The colleagues, friends, and mentors who reviewed various chapters of this book's manuscript, offering constructive feedback and challenging me, in turn helping the book's final shape take form. Their support, encouragement and insights were crucial! Thank you to: R' Aaron Bergman, R' Aaron Miller, R' Aaron Potek, R' Adam Greenwald, Alan Scher, Ali Duhan, Allan Nachman, R' Ari Moffic, Ariella Raviv, Arnie Sohinki, R' Asher Lopatin, R' Ben Herman, Cindy Hughey, R' Dana Saroken, R' Danny Syme, David Bryfman, David Cygielman, R' David Evan Markus, R' David Segal, Debbie Zeger, Diane Schilit, Elliot Darvick, R' Eric Solomon, R' Eric Yanoff, R' Eytan Kenter, Gary Wolff, George Roberts, Graham Hoffman, Prof. Howard Lupovitch, Igor Alterman, R' Jason Miller, R' Jeff Dreifus, R' Jeff Stombaugh, R' Jen Lader, Jeremy Shuback, Jesse Rosen, Joel Marcovitch, Jordan Fruchtman, R' Josh Foster, Laura Feldman Weiner, Leah Jones, R' Leonardo Bitran, R' Lex Rofeberg, Lisa Soble Siegmann, Marisa Meyerson, Matt Bonney-Cohen, R' Michael Knopf, R' Rachel Ain, R' Rachel Greengrass, Rachel Hodes, R' Rachel Kohl Finegold, Rebecca Weisman, Sarah Hurwitz, Sarah Schonberg, Sheri Horwitz, Shimon Levy, R' Sid Schwarz, Steven Davis, Tiffany Harris, Todd Rockoff, Yoni Sarason, and Zach Foster.

~ Those who made the time to review the entire book manuscript and pen blurbs: Dan Elbaum, Dr. David Bryfman, Doron Krakow, R' Elliot Cosgrove, R' Jen Gubitz, Kohenet Keshira HaLev Fife, R' Peter Rubenstein, R' Rachel Barenblat, R' Rachel Kohl Finegold, R' Rick Jacobs, Dr. Ron Wolfson, Sarah Hurwitz, R' Sid Schwarz, R' Terry Bookman and R' Yonatan Dahlen.

~ Prof. Ron Wolfson, Prof. Roberta Rosenthal Kwall, Rabbi Terry Bookman and Zack Bodner for your generosity and patience in guiding me through the book proposal and development process, and to Zack for writing the Afterword to the book as well.

~ Larry Yudelson and the Ben Yehuda Press team, for giving me the opportunity to channel my voice in this way.

~ Laura Logan and the RE:WORK Editing team, especially fellow Millennial Kira Schwartz, for your support and efforts during the editing process.

~ Adat Shalom Synagogue, for embracing me as part of your clergy team and for providing me with the space to write this book.

~ My grandparents:

Sally Horwitz, of blessed memory, who survived concentration camps and unspeakable horrors, and still managed to build a Jewish life full of laughter and love. She encouraged me to get a law degree because with it, I could do anything (like run a Jewish nonprofit). She was right.

Morton Horwitz, of blessed memory, who embraced and emphasized Jewish tradition, read everything he could get his hands on, engaged me in conversation regularly about the future of Jewish life, and was always ready to share a song.

Berta Wesler, who as a child, after Kristallnacht, was part of the Kindertransport, shipped from Germany to England where she was foster raised, never to see her parents and many of her other relatives again. An ardent Zionist, as a teen she moved to Israel and served in the *Haganah*, instilling her descendants with pride and love for the Jewish people and Israel.

Phil Wesler, who, legend has it, placed a violin in my crib at age 2 days, ensuring from my earliest moments that I'd have a love of making music, which serves as my spiritual core. The violin I play today belonged to him and his father before him and is my most treasured possession.

~ My parents, Arthur and Gina, for the incredible role models they have been, for making our Jewish family life joyous, and for all the ways they have invested in me. I simply would not be the person I am today without my parents, who are truly my closest friends and confidants. Not to mention the childcare hours they took on so that I had the space to write. They also each read every word of this book—multiple times—during the editing process. Mom and Dad, I love you. Thank you for granting me this blessed life.

~ My kiddos, Jonah, Micah and Atara. Thanks for choosing me to be your Abba. I hope one day you'll read this book and be proud of the work I did in your early years of life and be inspired to also go out and make your mark on the Jewish (and broader) world. You each have such a unique spirit, and I can't wait to watch you grow up. Please also remember when you read this paragraph as an adult that there was a period of time where your Abba and his work were deemed "hip" and "cool."

~ My partner in everything, Miriam Liora. There aren't enough pages to express how grateful I am to you, and for all you've done to support our family and me on this journey—often without fanfare or recognition. You are my *bashert*, and courtesy of having you as my partner, *kosi revaya*—my cup overflows. From the bottom of my heart, thank you. I love you.

Books Referenced

Alexander, Michelle. *The New Jim Crow* (The New Press, 2010)

Ariely, Dan. *Predictably Irrational* (Harper Collins, 2008)

Berman, Lila Corwin. *The American Jewish Philanthropic Complex* (Princeton University Press, 2020)

Bodner, Zack. *Why Do Jewish?* (Gefen Publishing House, 2021)

Bookman, Terry. *Beyond Survival* (Rowman & Littlefield, 2019)

Case, Edmund. *Radical Inclusion* (Center for Radically Inclusive Judaism, 2019)

Chazan, Barry A., et al., editors. *Israel: Voices from Within* (Third Place Publications, 2020)

Dorff, Elliot. *Conservative Judaism* (Youth Commission, United Synagogue of America, 1977)

Fishkoff, Sue. *The Rebbe's Army* (Schocken Books, 2003)

Gordis, Daniel. *We Stand Divided* (Ecco, 2019)

Green, Arthur. *Radical Judaism* (Yale University Press, 2010)

Handlarski, Denise. *The A-Z of Intermarriage* (New Jewish Press, 2020)

Heath, Chip, and Dan Heath. *The Power of Moments* (Simon and Schuster, 2017)

Herring, Hayim. *Tomorrow's Synagogue Today* (Rowman & Littlefield, 2012)

Heschel, Abraham J. *The Insecurity of Freedom* (Farrar, Straus and Giroux, 1966)

Hoffman, Warren, and Miriam Steinberg-Egeth. *Warm and Welcoming* (Rowman & Littlefield, 2021)

Hurwitz, Sarah. *Here All Along* (Random House, 2019)

Judson, Daniel. *Pennies for Heaven* (Brandeis University Press, 2019)

Kaunfer, Elie. *Empowered Judaism* (Jewish Lights, 2012)

Khoury, Raymond. *The Sign* (Berkley, 2010)

Kwall, Roberta Rosenthal. *Remix Judaism* (Rowman & Littlefield, 2022)

Lancaster, Lynn C., and David Stillman. *When Generations Collide* (Harper Business, 2003)

Levy, Naomi. *Einstein and the Rabbi* (Flatiron, 2018)

Mirvis, Jonathan. *It's Our Challenge* (YouCaxton Publications, 2016)

Mother Theresa. *No Greater Love* (New World Library, 2002)

Olitzky, Kerry M., *Playlist Judaism* (Rowman & Littlefield, 2013)

Olitzky, Kerry M., Avi S. Olitzky. *New Membership and Financial Alternatives for the American Synagogue* (Jewish Lights, 2015)

Parker, Priya. *The Art of Gathering* (Penguin, 2018)

Pink, Daniel H. *Drive* (Riverhead Books, 2011)

Pogrebin, Abigail. *My Jewish Year* (Fig Tree Books, 2017)

Prager, Marcia. *The Path of Blessing* (Jewish Lights, 2003)

Putnam, Robert D., *Bowling Alone* (Simon & Schuster, 2000)

Sacks, Jonathan. *Future Tense* (Schocken, 2012)

Sarna, Jonathan D. *American Judaism* (Yale University Press, 2004)

Schwarz, Sidney. *Finding a Spiritual Home* (Jewish Lights, 2003)

Schwarz, Sidney. *Jewish Megatrends* (Jewish Lights, 2013)

Shlain, Tiffany. *24/6* (Gallery Books, 2020)

Sonsino, Rifat, and Daniel B. Syme. *Finding God* (Union of American Hebrew Congregations, 1986)

Stanton, Joshua, and Benjamin Spratt. *Awakenings* (Behrman House, 2022)

Steinhardt, Michael. *Jewish Pride* (Wicked Son, 2022)

Tishby, Noa. *Israel* (Free Press, 2022)

Uram, Mike. *Next Generation Judaism* (Jewish Lights, 2016)

Wolfson, Ron. *Relational Judaism* (Jewish Lights, 2013)

Wolfson, Ron, and Brett Kopin. *Creating Sacred Communities* (The Kripke Institute, 2022)

Organizations Referenced

18Doors: 18doors.org
Adat Shalom Synagogue: adatshalom.org
Agudath Israel of America: agudah.org
Alper JCC Miami: alperjcc.org
American Jewish Joint Distribution Committee: jdc.org
Amplifier: amplifiergiving.org
At The Well: atthewellproject.com
Base: basemovement.org/
Birthright Israel: birthrightisrael.com
Camp Nai Nai Nai: campnainainai.org
Chabad: chabad.org
Covenant Foundation: covenantfn.org
Detroit Jews for Justice: detroitjewsforjustice.org
Friendseder: friendseder.com
GatherDC: gatherdc.org
Germany Close Up: germanycloseup.de
Hadar: hadar.org
Haggadot.com: haggadot.com
Hazon: hazon.org
Hillel International: hillel.org
Hillel Office of Innovation: ooi.us
Honeymoon Israel: honeymoonisrael.org
Immerse NYC: immersenyc.org
JDate: jdate.com
JDC Entwine: jdcentwine.org
Jewish Agency for Israel: jewishagency.org

Jewish Education Project: jewishedproject.org

Jewish Federation of Metropolitan Detroit: jewishdetroit.org

Jewish Federations of North America: jfna.org

Jewish Renewal: aleph.org

Jews of Color Initiative: jewsofcolorinitiative.org

JSwipe: jswipeapp.com

Judaism Unbound: judaismunbound.com

Keshet: keshetonline.org

Leading Edge: leadingedge.org

Lippman Kanfer Foundation for Living Torah: lklft.org

M2: The Institute for Experiential Jewish Education: ieje.org

Marlene Meyerson JCC: mmjccm.org

Michigan State University Hillel: msuhillel.org

Moishe House: moishehouse.org

OneTable: onetable.org

Open Dor Project: opendorproject.org

Orthodox Union: ou.org

Pardes Institute of Jewish Studies: pardes.org.il

Penn Hillel: pennhillel.org

PJ Library: pjlibrary.org

Reboot: rebooting.com

Reconstructing Judaism: reconstructingjudaism.org

Repair The World: werepair.org

Sinai and Synapses: sinaiandsynapses.org

Slingshot: slingshotfund.org

Society for Humanistic Judaism: shj.org

Svara: svara.org

Temple Israel: temple-israel.org

The Riverway Project: riverwayproject.org

The Soul Center: soulcenterbaltimore.org

The Well: meetyouatthewell.org

Trybal Gatherings: trybalgatherings.com

United Synagogue of Conservative Judaism: uscj.org

About The Author

Rabbi Dan Horwitz is committed to fostering a joyful Judaism that is inclusive, inspiring and relevant. A research-informed practitioner, in addition to rabbinic ordination, he holds a BA, three MAs and a JD. Now serving as the CEO of the Jewish Federation of Greater Nashville, he previously served as a rabbi of Adat Shalom Synagogue in Metro Detroit and as the CEO of the Alper JCC in Miami. Dan was the founding director and rabbi of The Well, which was repeatedly recognized as one of the most innovative Jewish organizations in North America. He also was the organizational rabbi for Moishe House, the global leader in engaging young Jewish adults in their 20s. Designated by the Jewish daily *Forward* as one of America's Most Inspiring Rabbis, Dan is lover of hummus, playing basketball, and Jewish music jam sessions. He makes his home in Nashville with his spouse Miriam and their three rambunctious children.

Reflections on the weekly Torah portion from *Ben Yehuda Press*

An Angel Called Truth and Other Tales from the Torah by Rabbi Jeremy Gordon and Emma Parlons. Funny, engaging micro-tales for each of the portions of the Torah and one for each of the Jewish festivals as well. These tales are told from the perspective of young people who feature in the Biblical narrative, young people who feature in classic Rabbinic commentary on our Biblical narratives and young people just made up for this book.

Torah & Company: The weekly portion of Torah, accompanied by generous helpings of Mishnah and Gemara, served with discussion questions to spice up your Sabbath Table by Rabbi Judith Z. Abrams. Serve up a rich feast of spiritual discussion from an age-old recipe: One part Torah. Two parts classic Jewish texts. Add conversation. Stir... and enjoy! "A valuable guide for the Shabbat table of every Jew." —Rabbi Burton L. Visotzky, author *Reading the Book*

Torah Journeys: The Inner Path to the Promised Land by Rabbi Shefa Gold. Rabbi Gold shows us how to find blessing, challenge and the opportunity for spiritual transformation in each portion of Torah. An inspiring guide to exploring the landscape of Scripture... and recognizing that landscape as the story of your life. "Deep study and contemplation went into the writing of this work. Reading her Torah teachings one becomes attuned to the voice of the Shekhinah, the feminine aspect of God which brings needed healing to our wounded world." —Rabbi Zalman Schachter-Shalomi

American Torah Toons 2: Fifty-Four Illustrated Commentaries by Lawrence Bush. Deeply personal and provocative artworks responding to each weekly Torah portion. Each two-page spread includes a Torah passage, a paragraph of commentary from both traditional and modern Jewish sources, and a photo-collage that responds to the text with humor, ethical conscience, and both social and self awareness. "What a vexing, funny, offensive, insightful, infuriating, thought-provoking book." —Rabbi David Saperstein

The Comic Torah: Reimagining the Very Good Book. Stand-up comic Aaron Freeman and artist Sharon Rosenzweig reimagine the Torah with provocative humor and irreverent reverence in this hilarious, gorgeous, off-beat graphic version of the Bible's first five books! Each weekly portion gets a two-page spread. Like the original, the Comic Torah is not always suitable for children.

we who desire: poems and Torah riffs by Sue Swartz. From Genesis to Deuteronomy, from Bereshit to Zot Haberacha, from Eden to Gaza, from Eve to Emma Goldman, *we who desire* interweaves the mythic and the mundane as it follows the arc of the Torah with carefully chosen words, astute observations, and deep emotion. "Sue Swartz has used a brilliant, fortified, playful, serious, humanely furious moral imagination, and a poet's love of the music of language, to re-tell the saga of the Bible you thought you knew." —Alicia Ostriker, author, *For the Love of God: The Bible as an Open Book*

Eternal Questions by Rabbi Josh Feigelson. These essays on the weekly Torah portion guide readers on a journey that weaves together Torah, Talmud, Hasidic masters, and a diverse array of writers, poets, musicians, and thinkers. Each essay includes questions for reflection and suggestions for practices to help turn study into more mindful, intentional living. "This is the wisdom that we always need—but maybe particularly now, more than ever, during these turbulent times." —Rabbi Danya Ruttenberg, author, *On Repentance and Repair*

Jewish spirituality and thought from *Ben Yehuda Press*

The Essential Writings of Abraham Isaac Kook. Translated and edited by Rabbi Ben Zion Bokser. This volume of letters, aphorisms and excerpts from essays and other writings provide a wide-ranging perspective on the thought and writing of Rav Kook. With most selections running two or three pages, readers gain a gentle introduction to one of the great Jewish thinkers of the modern era.

Ahron's Heart: Essential Prayers, Teachings and Letters of Ahrele Roth, a Hasidic Reformer. Translated and edited by Rabbi Zalman Schachter-Shalomi and Rabbi Yair Hillel Goelman. For the first time, the writings of one of the 20th century's most important Hasidic thinkers are made available to a non-Hasidic English audience. Rabbi Ahron "Ahrele" Roth (1894-1944) has a great deal to say to sincere spiritual seekers far beyond his own community.

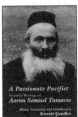

A Passionate Pacifist: Essential Writings of Aaron Samuel Tamares. Translated and edited by Rabbi Everett Gendler. Rabbi Aaron Samuel Tamares (1869-1931) addresses the timeless issues of ethics, morality, communal morale, and Judaism in relation to the world at large in these essays and sermons, written in Hebrew between 1904 and 1931. "For those who seek a Torah of compassion and pacifism, a Judaism not tied to 19th century political nationalism, and a vision of Jewish spirituality outside of political thinking this book will be essential." —Rabbi Dr. Alan Brill, author, *Thinking God: The Mysticism of Rabbi Zadok of Lublin*

Return to the Place: The Magic, Meditation, and Mystery of Sefer Yetzirah by Rabbi Jill Hammer. A translation of and commentary to an ancient Jewish mystical text that transforms it into a contemporary guide for meditative practice. "A tour de force—at once scholarly, whimsical, deeply poetic, and eminently accessible." —Rabbi Tirzah Firestone, author of *The Receiving: Reclaiming Jewish Women's Wisdom*

Enlightenment by Trial and Error: Ten Years on the Slippery Slopes of Jewish Mysticism, Postmodern Buddhist Meditation, and Heretical Flexidox Spirituality by Rabbi Jay Michaelson. A unique record of the 21st century spiritual search, from the perspective of someone who made plenty of mistakes along the way.

The Tao of Solomon: Finding Joy and Contentment in the Wisdom of Ecclesiastes by Rabbi Rami Shapiro. Rabbi Rami Shapiro unravels the golden philosophical threads of wisdom in the book of Ecclesiastes, reweaving the vibrant book of the Bible into a 21st century tapestry. Shapiro honors the roots of the ancient writing, explores the timeless truth that we are merely a drop in the endless river of time, and reveals a path to finding personal and spiritual fulfillment even as we embrace our impermanent place in the universe.

Embracing Auschwitz: Forging a Vibrant, Life-Affirming Judaism that Takes the Holocaust Seriously by Rabbi Joshua Hammerman. The Judaism of Sinai and the Judaism of Auschwitz are merging, resulting in new visions of Judaism that are only beginning to take shape. "Should be read by every Jew who cares about Judaism." —Rabbi Dr. Irving "Yitz" Greenberg

Recent books from *Ben Yehuda Press*

Reaching for Comfort: What I Saw, What I Learned, and How I Blew it Training as a Pastoral Counselor by Sherri Mandell. In 2004, Sherri Mandell won the National Jewish Book award for *The Blessing of the Broken Heart*, which told of her grief and initial mourning after her 13-year-old son Koby was brutally murdered. Years later, with her pain still undiminished, Sherri trains to help others as a pioneering pastoral counselor in Israeli hospitals. "What a blessing to witness Mandell's and her patients' resilience!" —Rabbi Dayle Friedman, editor, *Jewish Pastoral Care: A Practical Guide from Traditional and Contemporary Sources*

Heroes with Chutzpah: 101 True Tales of Jewish Trailblazers, Changemakers & Rebels by Rabbi Deborah Bodin Cohen and Rabbi Kerry Olitzky. Readers ages 8 to 14 will meet Jewish changemakers from the recent past and present, who challenged the status quo in the arts, sciences, social justice, sports and politics, from David Ben-Gurion and Jonas Salk to Sarah Silverman and Douglas Emhoff. "Simply stunning. You would want this book on your coffee table, though the stories will take the express lane to your soul." —Rabbi Jeff Salkin

Just Jewish: How to Engage Millennials and Build a Vibrant Jewish Future by Rabbi Dan Horwitz. Drawing on his experience launching The Well, an inclusive Jewish community for young adults in Metro Detroit, Rabbi Horwitz shares proven techniques ready to be adopted by the Jewish world's myriad organizations, touching on everything from branding to fundraising to programmatic approaches to relationship development, and more. "This book will shape the conversation as to how we think about the Jewish future." —Rabbi Elliot Cosgrove, editor, *Jewish Theology in Our Time*.

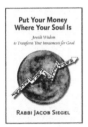

Put Your Money Where Your Soul Is: Jewish Wisdom to Transform Your Investments for Good by Rabbi Jacob Siegel. "An intellectual delight. It offers a cornucopia of good ideas, institutions, and advisers. These can ease the transition for institutions and individuals from pure profit nature investing to deploying one's capital to repair the world, lift up the poor, and aid the needy and vulnerable. The sources alone—ranging from the Bible, Talmud, and codes to contemporary economics and sophisticated financial reporting—are worth the price of admission." —Rabbi Irving "Yitz" Greenberg

Why Israel (and its Future) Matters: Letters of a Liberal Rabbi to the Next Generation by Rabbi John Rosove. Presented in the form of a series of letters to his children, Rabbi Rosove makes the case for Israel — and for liberal American Jewish engagement with the Jewish state. "A must-read!" —Isaac Herzog, President of Israel. "This thoughtful and passionate book reminds us that commitment to Israel and to social justice are essential components of a healthy Jewish identity." —Yossi Klein Halevi, author, *Letters to My Palestinian Neighbor*

Other Covenants: Alternate Histories of the Jewish People by Rabbi Andrea D. Lobel & Mark Shainblum. In *Other Covenants*, you'll meet Israeli astronauts trying to save a doomed space shuttle, a Jewish community's faith challenged by the unstoppable return of their own undead, a Jewish science fiction writer in a world of Zeppelins and magic, an adult Anne Frank, an entire genre of Jewish martial arts movies, a Nazi dystopia where Judaism refuses to die, and many more. Nominated for two Sidewise Awards for Alternate History.

Made in the USA
Columbia, SC
05 February 2024

31500175R00127